A Thousand Miles in the Rob Roy Canoe

on the Rivers and Lakes of Europe

By J. MacGregor, M.A.

Captain of the Royal Canoe Club

Dixon-Price Publishing,

Murray, Utah

First printed in 1866 in London, England.

This edition is based upon the 21st edition, published in 1892 by Sampson Low, Marlowe & Company, London, England. Spelling and punctuation have been updated to reflect modern usage, but otherwise the text is unchanged. Volume arrangement Copyright© 2000 by Dixon-Price Publishing, Murray, Utah.

No part of this book may be copied for commercial use without the permission of the publisher.

MacGregor, John, 1825-1892.
   A thousand miles in the Rob Roy canoe on the lakes and rivers of Europe / by J. MacGregor.
   p. cm.
   Originally published: London : Sampson, Low, Marlowe, 1892. 21st ed.
   ISBN 1-929516-0601
    1. History—Miscellanea. 2. Europe—Description and travel. 3. MacGregor, John, 1825-1892—Journeys—Europe. 4. Canoes and canoeing—Europe. I. Title

D919 .H642 2000
914.04'286—dc21

                                 99-086904

ISBN 1-929516-06-1

Printed in the U.S.A. by Lightning Print, Inc., LaVergne, Tenn.

Dixon-Price Publishing
618 West Spacerama, Ste. 100
Murray, UT 84123

CONTENTS

Introduction by Brian Kologe 5

CHAPTER I 13
The Canoeist—Other Modes—The Rob Roy—Handbook—Hints—The Dress—The Role

CHAPTER II 20
The Start—The Thames—Flies—Under Sail—Porpoises—A Noreaster—Sailing on the Sea—On the Meuse—Barriers and Shallows—Huy—Gunbarrels—Earl of Aberdeen—A Drowning Boy—Swimmers—A Night Climb—The Premier's Son—Nothing to Pay—A Day's Sail—Downhill—Canoes and Cannons—The Prince of Wales—Alone again.

CHAPTER III 39
Höllenthal Pass—Lady Friends—Night Music—Manners—Pontius Pilate—A Schwartzwald Storm—Starers—The Singers—Donaueschingen—Banket—An English Groom—Waiterdom—Source of the Danube—Its Name

CHAPTER IV 51
The Danube—"Guten Tag"—Canoe Pleasures—All R-r-r-ight—The Weed—Shooting a dam—Day's delights—Toy Barrow—Tuttlingen—The Crowds—The Monastery—Melanie—Tracts—Monks' Cowls—Distance travelled—Reflections

CHAPTER V 67
Panting Visitors—Hohenzollern—Roman Nose—Herons in Council—Among the Haymakers—Boating Boy—Winged Music—Arched Chasms—Hidden Song—Navvies—Different Dangers—A Gale—Hungry Nap—Chasing a Church—Snags in Darkness—The Vagrant—Classics—Hotel Bills

CHAPTER VI 83
Daydream—Ulm—River Iller—Bismarck's Besom—Fredrickshafen—Lake Constance—Idiots—A Wiseacre—On Rhine again—Goosewinged—Sign speech—Gasthaus—With an Arab—Water bewitched—The Emperor—How to Moor—Grand Duchy again—By the Moon—The Idlers

CHAPTER VII 100
Fog Picture—Boy Soldiers—Schaffhausen Falls—Eating—Bachelor's Fare—Lake of Zurich—Like a Dog—Crinoline—Spectators—Lake of Zug—Swiss Riflemen—Mist Curtains—Sailing—Fishing Britons—Flogging the Water—Odd Britons—Talk-books—A Suggestion.

CHAPTER VIII 117
Lake of Lucerne—Seeburg Hotel—Bonâ-fide Bite—The Rapid Reuss—Fair Friends—Is it right?—Caught by a Rope—Barriers—The Hard Place—Din—Headlong—The Struggle—Bremgarten

CHAPTER IX 129
    Hunger—Music at the Mill—Damsels—Sentiment and
        Chops—Buying Clothes—The Snags—Shooting a Fall—Fixed—
        An ex-Courier—Log Bearings—The Drowned Lord—"Wasserfall"—Cow
        and Canoe—"Valtare Scote"—"Man Preserver."
CHAPTER X 142
    A Field of Foam—Precipice—Puzzled—Philosophy—Rheinfelden Rapids—
        Dazzled—Jabbering—Blissful Ignorance—Astride—Find a Way—Very
        Salt—Bright Lad—German Friend—The Whirlpool—Cauliflower—
        Bride and Baby—"Squar."
CHAPTER XI 156
    Which way?—Music in Jungle—Byron—Drawbridges—Gros Kembs
        Thunderer—Thoroughly dull—Fifty Locks—The Bother at them—
        Thoughts—An odd Fish—Night Notes—Madame Nico—Tedious—
        Stared at—The Lady Cow—New Wine
CHAPTER XII 170
    River Thur—Fire! Fire!—Over the Vosges—"Th"—Popish Pilgrims—Source of
        the Moselle—Remiremont—Launched on the Moselle—Lovely Scenes—
        The Paddle—Spell-bound—Washerwomen—Graceful Salute—Run away
        with—Policemen.
CHAPTER XIII 183
    River Moselle—The Tramp—Battery of Blessings—Halcyon—Painted Woman
        —Sad Loss—Very Shabby—In a Hedge—A Discovery—River
        Meurthe—Flirting—Ducks—A Moving House—A Mother's Tears—
        Night Frolic—Salt Mine—Work for the Young
CHAPTER XIV 198
    Luxuries—Monks—Camp at Chalons—Inns of Court—A Widower—Leaks—
        Come to see a Smash—Champagne—The River Marne—Name of my
        Wife—Silence—The Sun—Rafts and Flocks—Newspapers—Millstones—
        Hot Wind—Old Soldier
CHAPTER XV 213
    Blacksmith—Holy Water—Quaint Questions —Unprotected Female—Grave
        Gazers—Wrong Ways—The Boys, the Boys—Bends of the Marne—Last
        Mooring—The Seine—Paris—Home.

Introduction by Brian Kologe

Had there been such a thing as a best-seller list in London in 1866, the eccentric volume you hold in your hands would probably have headed it. Modestly described by its author as "the log of a charming cruise in a small Canoe," it single-handedly created a rage for what came to be known as canoeing in Britain and kayaking in the United States.

A Thousand Miles in the Rob Roy Canoe, closely followed by *The Rob Roy on the Baltic* (1867) and *The Rob Roy on the Jordan* (1869), made John MacGregor a household word in Britain. Ironically, almost 140 years later – with kayakers paddling waters from the antipodes to the equator – MacGregor's books have languished out of print for decades. The man anointed the "patron saint of canoeing" has almost disappeared over the horizon.

Just as Izaak Walton's contemplative *Compleat Angler* sent generations to the water's edge with hook and line, *A Thousand Miles in the Rob Roy Canoe* launched countless paddlers down the pathless avenues of stream, river, lake, and ocean. To the uninitiated, MacGregor's exuberance may seem exaggerated, but to those who know them, kayaks inspire nothing short of reverence. They embody simplicity, elegance, maneuverability, comfort, and seaworthiness. They will float in water just deep enough to wet one's ankles and yet, as Franz Romer demonstrated in 1928 and Hannes Lindemann in 1957, they are capable of crossing oceans. In calm conditions, propelling one requires less effort than that other most benign of conveyances, the bicycle.

Although his writings encouraged numerous adventurers to wet their keels, MacGregor's books also floated a small navy of armchair paddlers. "I am so very well acquainted with the *Rob Roy* canoe," Charles Dickens would write MacGregor, "and have taken passage in her with so much pleasure."

MacGregor's fame as a canoeist came more than midway in a life, which in the most understated recounting, sounds like a fictional chronicle of two, maybe three lives penned by Robert Louis Stevenson. The son of General Sir Duncan MacGregor who fought against Napoleon, John MacGregor was an adventurer from the outset. In 1825, only three-months-old, he was rescued with his parents from a burning ship in which they had set sail for India. MacGregor returned the favor as a 12-year-old, helping launch a rescue boat bound for a ship in distress off Belfast, Ireland, then slipping aboard unnoticed at the last instant.

His childhood was an improbable mixture of piety, mischief, and adventure, full of sailing, boat-building, tree-climbing, reading, riding, boxing, and shooting. A youthful companion recalled John's aptitude for mechanics, his homemade steam engines, electrical machines, galvanic batteries, and especially his "intolerable chemical mixtures which resulted in several rather serious explosions."

His father's frequent reassignments led him down the corridors of seven schools before he graduated Trinity College, Dublin in 1839 with a degree in mathematics. At Cambridge, he subsequently studied patent law. Even before his kayaking escapades, he'd toured Europe, the Middle East, Russia, and North Africa, and later the United States, Canada, and Siberia. These outings included bouts with fever, hand-to-hand combat with Greek pirates and Arab brigands, and tangles with crocodiles, storms, and jackals. He ascended Mont Blanc, Etna, and Vesuvius. He headed a company of Scots volunteers in London, won three awards for sharpshooting, drew for Punch, and wrote for the *Mechanics Maga-*

zine. He published an exhaustive book on marine propulsion, two on patent law, several on travel, and one which transcribed Syrian and Egyptian melodies he had heard in the Middle East. He illustrated not only his own books but explorer David Livingstone's *Travels and Researches in South Africa*.

While he was acquainted with such well known figures as Bishop Wilberforce, Mathew Arnold, Thomas Carlyle, and painter John Everett Millais, he never lost what Kipling called the common touch. Seeing a house fire from his window one day in London, he raced to it and lent his considerable vigor to the firemen's pump, enjoying their company afterward over a post-conflagration beer.

Although MacGregor neither invented nor discovered the kayak — specimens first arrived in England with Martin Frobisher in the 16th century – he seems to have been the first European to appreciate and advertise its virtues. As early as 1848 he had been intrigued by an India-rubber vessel which simultaneously served as a "cloak, tent, boat and bed." Three years later, touring Siberia and Canada, he was further impressed by aboriginal skin boats. In 1865 he commissioned Searles of Lambeth to construct to his specifications the first in a series of seven clinker-built, cedar and oak "canoes," each of which he christened "Rob Roy." The original, which weighed 80 pounds and was equipped with a lugsail and jib as well as a seven-foot double-bladed paddle, is now preserved in the National Maritime Museum in Greenwich, England. It measures 15-feet-long with a 28-inch beam, is nine inches deep, and draws a scant three inches. A later incarnation which MacGregor took to the Middle East, was modified to include a removable rear deck, allowing him to rig a tent fly, drop mosquito netting, and indeed, sleep aboard.

While MacGregor's first 600 converts formed the Royal

Canoe Club, with H.R.H. Edward, Prince of Wales as commodore, kayaking was not merely a sport of Kings. Because kayaks could be built by amateurs or purchased for reasonable prices, they would soon earn a reputation as "the poor man's yacht."

Since MacGregor's day, kayaks have undergone modifications in design and materials, have been traced back to their aboriginal origins and projected forward with Computer-Aided Design, yet the fundamental experience remains surprisingly unchanged. The kayak's greatest virtue, the one most amplified in MacGregor's work, is its ability to escape modern life, to embark on an adventure as proximate as the nearest body of water or half a world away. The Rob Roy is, above all, a tranquil vantage point allowing an unobstructed view of wildlife and shore life. It is below the level of nearby roads and lower than the gunwales of anything else afloat. Perhaps the democratic nature of this frugal pastime or the vision of gentlemen—even ladies—splashing about in humble vessels, led some of MacGregor's contemporaries to rail against the "upstart phenomenon."

"It is the invention of savages," hissed one critic, lampooning MacGregor as a kind of aquatic centaur afloat in a "damp tub": "It is necessity, not choice or pleasure which justifies recourse to such an imperfect, unscientific, uncomfortable imitation of the true boat. We say it is a species of mockery to go on expeditions of length and cost in a craft whose only method of propulsion is based on the most wasteful expenditure of man's powers ever invented." To others the most disturbing aspect was what sort of impression this odd example of British manhood, this floating ambassador sans portfolio, made on the Continent. Some readers accuse MacGregor of chauvinism; the truth is he never missed an opportunity to tweak the stodgier specimens of his own nation.

In any case, in the summer of 1865, lighting his cigar and buoyant in every sense, MacGregor set off down the Thames, waving merrily to astonished bargemen then venturing into the Channel where he found himself surrounded by a pod of porpoises. Passing her sea-trials, the Rob Roy was ferried to the Continent where she traveled by train and occasionally oxcart to the headwaters and shores of various rivers and lakes in France, Germany, Switzerland, and Belgium.

The object of it all, MacGregor would write, was "a new mode of travelling on the Continent by which new people and things are met with, while healthy exercise is enjoyed and an interest ever varied with excitement keeps fully alert the energies of the mind."

As the embodiment of this new independent traveler, MacGregor was impervious to the blandishments of hired guides or the security of Cook's Tours. He set off for the entire summer with a spirit stove, a wooden fork and spoon (cunningly carved at opposite ends of the same stem), one spare button, and nine pounds of luggage. While his kit might be Spartan, fitting together "like the words in hexameter verse," MacGregor decked himself out in a gray flannel Norfolk jacket ("garnished with six pockets"), matching trousers, canvas wading shoes, blue spectacles, and a straw boater — a diminutive silk Union Jack for the boat.

To say this six-foot-six vision of sartorial splendor enjoyed creating an effect, whether in life or upon the page, would be an understatement. Because his trips were widely publicized, shipping frequently altered course for a closer look and ashore he received plentiful offers of meals and lodging. Even when unrecognized, gliding down the Meuse in Belgium, the Rob Roy precipitated a mild sensation. "When the little steamer passed I drew along side and got my penny roll and penny glass of beer through the porthole, while the wondering passengers smiled, chattered, and then looked grave – for was it not indecorous to laugh at an Englishman evidently mad, poor fellow?"

Nor is he above an occasional prank. Paddling unseen below the Danube's banks, he indulges a hearty chorus of "Rule Britannia" much to the bafflement of peasants cutting hay nearby. To break the ice and the language barrier, MacGregor often produced his sketch pad and showed all and sundry the record of his travels, or, when all else failed he would ignite a strip of magnesium ribbon carried for such occasions, playing to a more easily entertained audience than one might find a century later.

MacGregor is not introspective nor confessional like say, Paul Theroux, whose *Happy Isles of Oceania* occupies the far end of kayaking's narrow bookshelf. He is, however, still eminently readable, his dry humor surviving intact. There are times when his tongue-in-cheek account of the enterprise approaches self-parody, becoming something like a "Monty Python" send-up of the Victorian sportsman, describing Europe as if he were Livingstone exploring the Zambezi. Were a film version of MacGregor's life produced today, casting would be a hard call – Sean Connery or John Cleese?

Despite occasional plunges down rapids or through a millrace, most of the book is a lazy idyll down the Danube, the Rhine, and numerous smaller streams. It gives the modern reader an unobstructed view of the tranquil vistas of 19th century Europe. The smooth flow of his prose lulls us down whole chapters of kingfishers, barge traffic, washerwomen, curious onlookers, jumping trout, picturesque stone bridges and quaint riverside inns — what seem, if not always familiar certainly common enough not to surprise us. Eventually, however, snagging on some detail, we awake with a start, remembering that all this is taking place before the Great War, before the internal combustion engine, the telephone or even household electricity. A window abruptly opens on a harbor full of gaff-rigged work-boats or a steam powered paddle wheeler. Streets clatter with horses. Bullocks pull carts. Bismarck's ominous troops drill or practice mock assaults on old fortresses.

Where MacGregor occasionally may try our patience is in his religious asides. He sincerely traced his faith to a boyhood incident, to praying for a fish while angling and having his prayer answered. A thwarted vocation for missionary work led MacGregor, who styled himself the "Chaplain of the Canoe," to distribute reams of Protestant tracts to surprised bystanders, and to make less than generous remarks concerning the "benighted" Roman Church. A satirical magazine portrayed MacGregor as a "tourist of the most terrible and portentous species – the tourist Evangelo-tractual," yet acknowledged him as a "first-rate oarsman." Overall, his rectitude is not overbearing and takes a backseat to his proselytizing the gospel of the canoe.

On the other hand, MacGregor did not merely espouse what he described as his "muscular Christianity," he lived it. The *Dictionary of National Biography* identifies him primarily as a philanthropist, and as the reader may notice, he donated the proceeds from *A Thousand Miles in the Rob Roy Canoe* to the Shipwrecked Mariner's Society and the Royal National Lifeboat Institution. For decades he expended his greatest energies educating and bettering the lot of London's downtrodden. He was vice-president of the Ragged-School Union, and — a firm believer in dignity and self-reliance — he initiated a Shoe-Black Brigade and a messenger service which employed destitute children. Combining two improbable interests, he raised money for charity by giving public lectures, hamming it up on stage with the Rob Roy, going off stage for a quick change into his canoeing outfit (or after the Jordan expedition, into a burnoose) and reappearing to wild cheers. "His natural genius for publicity," wrote Arthur Ransome, "his instinctive showmanship, was always of service to whatever cause he might happen to be advocating."

In 1873, after his first lecture tour, MacGregor boarded a ship for the Azores with the latest Rob Roy, but the expedition was never completed. He turned around for England, driving directly to propose to Annie Caffin, who he had loved "eight years in silence," and astounding many who regarded him as a confirmed bachelor. They had two daughters, and though his charitable work continued, failing health ended his life as an adventurer.

Two years after he died in 1892, Edwin Hodder, his biographer, would describe him as "an original traveler, striking out new methods for himself, taking his own views of men, progress and things, and telling with boyish frankness what he thought and felt." For today's reader, MacGregor can be wonderfully tonic, an antidote to all our overly easy cynicism, an inspiring man who jumped into everything that came his way with contagious enthusiasm.

"It is, as in the voyage of life," MacGregor wrote in *A Thousand Miles in the Rob Roy Canoe*, "that each care and hardship is a very Mentor of living. Our minds would only vegetate if all life were like a straight canal, and we in a boat being towed along it. The afflictions that agitate the soul are as its shallows, rocks, and whirlpools, and the bark that has not been tossed on billows knows not half the sweetness of the harbor of rest."

Brian Kologe, 2000

CHAPTER I

*The Canoeist—Other Modes—The Rob Roy
—Handbook—Hints—The Dress—The Role*

A smash in a railway carriage one day hurled me under the seat, entangled in broken telegraph wires. No worse came of it than a shake of those nerves which one needs for rifle shooting; but as the bull's-eyes at a thousand yards were thereby made to few on the target, I turned in one night back again to my life on the water in boyish glee, and dreamed a new cruise, and planned a new craft, on my pillow.

It was clear that no rowboat would serve on a land-water voyage of this sort, for in the wildest parts of the best rivers the channel is too narrow for oars, or, if wide enough, it is often too shallow; and the tortuous passages, the rocks and banks, the weeds and snags, the milldams, barriers, fallen trees, rapids, whirlpools, and waterfalls that constantly occur on a river winding among hills make those very parts where the scenery is wildest and best to be quite unapproachable in such a boat, for it would be swamped by the sharp waves, or upset over the sunken rocks, which cannot be seen by a steersman.

Now these very things which bother the "pair oar," become cheery excitements to the voyager in a canoe. For now, as he sits in his little bark, he looks forward, and not backward. He sees all his course, and the scenery besides. With one sweep of his paddle he can turn aside when only a foot from destruction. He can steer within an inch in a narrow place, and can easily pass through reeds and weeds, or branches and grass; can work his sail without changing his seat; can shove with his paddle when aground, and can jump out in good time to prevent a bad smash. He can wade and haul his craft over the shallows, or drag it on dry ground, through the fields and hedges, over dykes, barriers, and walls; can carry it by hand up ladders and stairs, and can transport his canoe over high mountains and broad plains in a cart drawn by a man, a horse, or a cow.

Besides all this, the covered canoe is far stronger than an open boat, and may be fearlessly dropped into a deep pool, a lock, or a millrace, and when the breakers are high in the open sea or in river rapids, they can only wash over the deck of a canoe, while it is always dry within.

The canoe is also safer than a rowing-boat, because you sit so low in it, and never require to shift your place or lose hold of the paddle; while for comfort during long hours, for days and weeks of hard work, the canoe is evidently the best, because you lean all the time against a swinging backboard, and when the paddle rests on your lap you are at ease as in an arm-chair; so that, while drifting along with the current or the wind, you can gaze around, and eat or read, or sketch, or chat with the starers on the bank, and yet, in a moment of sudden alarm, the hands are at once on the faithful paddle ready for action.

Finally, you can lie at full length in the canoe, with a sail

A Thousand Miles in the Rob Roy Canoe

as an awning for the sun, or a shelter for rain, and you can sleep at night under its cover, or inside it when made for that purpose, with at least as much room for turning in your bed as sufficed for the great Duke of Wellington; or, if you are tired of the water for a time, you can leave your boat at an inn—where it will not be "eating its head off," like a horse; or you can send it home, or sell it, and take to the road yourself, or sink back again into the lazy cushions of a first-class carriage, and dream you are seeing the world.

But it may well be asked from one who thus praises the paddle, "Has he travelled in other ways, so as to know their several pleasures? Has he climbed glaciers and volcanoes, dived into caves and catacombs, trotted in the Norway carriole, ambled on an Arab and galloped on the Russian steppes? Does he know the charms of a Nile boat, or a Trinity Eight, or a Yankee steamer, or a sail in the Ægean, or a mule in Spain? Has he swung upon a camel, or glided in a sleigh, or sailed a yacht, or trundled in a Rantoone?"

Yes, he has thoroughly enjoyed these and other modes of locomotion, fast and slow. And now having used the canoe in Europe, Asia, Africa, and America, he finds the pleasure of the paddle is the best of them all.

With such advantages, then, and with good weather and good health, the canoe voyage about to be described was truly delightful.

This was the first such cruise, but many others followed. You may see a list of them in the "Canoeist," published by the Royal Canoe Club, of which the Prince of Wales is Commodore, with six hundred members, in all parts of the world.

The Rob Roy Canoe was built of oak, with a deck of cedar. She was made just short enough to go into the German railway wagons; that is to say, fifteen feet in length, twenty-eight inches broad, nine inches wide, and weighed eighty pounds. My baggage for three months was in a black bag, one foot square and six inches deep. A paddle seven feet long, with a blade at each end, and a lug sail and jib, were the means of propulsion; and a pretty blue silk Union Jack was the only ornament.[1]

But, having got this little boat, the difficulty was to find where she could go to, or what rivers were at once feasible to paddle on and pretty to see.

Inquiries in London as to this had no result. Even the Paris Boat Club knew nothing of French rivers. The Rhine they knew but only as a wished-for boundary, and it was soon pretty plain that, after quitting the Rhine, my cruise must be a voyage of discovery. Let us hope, then, that this narrative will lessen the trouble, while it stimulates the desire, of the numerous travellers who spend their vacation aboard a canoe.[2]

Not that I shall attempt to make a "handbook" to any of these streams. The man who has a spark of enterprise would turn from a river of which every reach was mapped and its channels duly lettered. Fancy the free traveller, equipped for a delicious summer of savage life, quietly submitting to be cramped and tutored by a "Chart of the Upper Mosel" in the style of the following extract, which is copied literally from a guidebook:—

(1) "Turn to the r. (right), cross the brook, and ascend by a broad and steep forest track (in 40 min.) to the hamlet of Albersbach, situate in the midst of verdant meadows. In five min. more a cross is reached, where the path to the l. must be taken; in 10 min. to the r., in the hollow, to the saw mill; in 10 min. more through the gate to the r.: in 3 min. the least trodden path to the l. leading to the Gaschpels Hof; after ¼ hr. the stony track into the wood must be ascended," &c., &c.—*From B—'s Rhine, p. 94.*

A Thousand Miles in the Rob Roy Canoe

Yet this sort of guide-book is not to be ridiculed. It is useful for some travellers as a ruled copy-book is of use to some writers. For first tours it may be needful and pleasant to have all made smooth and easy, to be carried in steamers or railways like a parcel, to stop at hotels full of English guests, and to ride, walk, or drive among people who know quite well already just what you will want to eat, and see, and do.

Year after year it is enough of excitement to some tourists to be shifted in squads from town to town, according to the routine of an excursion ticket. Those who are a little more advanced will venture to devise a tour from the mazy pages of Bradshaw, and with portmanteau and bag, and hat-box and sticks, they find more than enough judgment and tact is needed when they arrive in a night-train abroad, and must fix on an omnibus in a strange town. Safe at last in the bedroom of the hotel, they exclaim with a sigh, "Well, here we are all right at last!"

But after mountains and caves, churches and galleries, ruins and battle-fields, have been pretty well seen, and after tact and fortitude have been educated by experience, the tourist is ready for at first more worry than pleasure, and these he will find in deeper searches among the natural scenery and national character of the very countries he has only skimmed before.

The rivers and streams on the continent are scarcely known to the English tourist, and all the beauty and life upon them no one has well seen.

In his Guide-book route, indeed, from town to town, the tourist has crossed this and that stream—has admired a few yards of the water, and has then left it forever. He is carried again on a noble river by night in a steamboat, or is whisked along its banks in a railway, and between two tunnels he gets a moment's glimpse at the lovely water, and lo! it is gone.

But a mine of rich beauty remains there to be explored, and fresh gems of life and character are waiting there to be gathered. These are not mapped and labelled and ticketed in any handbook yet, and far better so, for the enjoyment of such treasures is enhanced to the best traveller by the energy and pluck required to get at them.

On this new world of waters, then, we are to launch the boat, the man, and his baggage, for we must describe all three, "Arma virumque canoe."

So what sort of dress did he wear?

My clothes for this tour consisted of a complete suit of grey flannel for use in the boat, and another suit of light but ordinary dress for shore and Sundays.

The "Norfolk jacket" is a loose frock-coat, like a blouse, with shoulder-straps, and belted at the waist, and garnished by six pockets.[3] With this excellent new-fashioned coat, a something in each of its pockets, and a Cambridge straw hat, canvas wading shoes, blue spectacles, a waterproof overcoat, and my spare jib for a sun shawl, there was sure to be a full day's enjoyment defiance of rain or sun, deeps or shallows, hunger or *ennui*.

Four hours' work to begin, and after them three of rest or floating, reading or sailing, and again a three hours' heavy pull, and then with a swim in the river or a bath at the inn, a change of garments, and a pleasant walk, all was made quite fresh again for a lively evening, a hearty dinner, pleasant talk, books, pictures, letters, and bed.

All being ready, and the weather very hot, at the end of July, when the country had caught the election fever, and M.P.'s went to scramble for seats, and the lawyers to thicken

A Thousand Miles in the Rob Roy Canoe

the bustle, and the last bullet at Wimbledon came "thud" on the target, it was time for the Rob Roy to start.

NOTES

1 After the cruise the author had a better canoe constructed, shorter and narrower (but with the same name), and in her he voyaged through Sweden, Norway and Denmark, Holstein, and some German waters.

The account of this voyage is given in *The Rob Roy on the Baltic*. The recent improvements of the canoe are described in that book, with woodcuts. The full description of a third canoe for sleeping in during a six months' voyage is given in *The Rob Roy on the Jordan, Nile, Red Sea, and Gennesareth*, a canoe cruise in Palestine and Egypt and the waters of the Damascus. A fourth canoe was used in the Zuyder Zee and among the isles of Holland and the Friesland coast; and the latest Rob Roy (Number 7) ran through the Shetland Isles and the Orkneys, and Scotch lakes.

2 The best German and Austrian maps were found to be frequently wrong. They showed villages on the banks which I found were a mile away in a wood, and so they were useless to one who had made up his mind (a good resolve) never to leave his boat.

3 This same suit went also through the second, third, and fourth voyages without a button damaged.

CHAPTER II

The Start—The Thames—Flies—Under Sail—Porpoises—A Noreaster—Sailing on the Sea—On the Meuse—Barriers and Shallows—Huy—Gun-barrels—Earl of Aberdeen—A Drowning Boy—Swimmers—A Night Climb—The Premier's Son—Nothing to Pay—A Day's Sail—Downhill—Canoes and Cannons—The Prince of Wales—Alone again.

The Rob Roy bounded away joyously on the top of the tide through Westminster Bridge, and swiftly shooting Blackfriars, she danced along the waves of the Pool, which looked all golden in the morning sun, but were in fact of pea-soup hue.

A fine breeze at Greenwich filled the new white sail, and we skimmed along with a cheery hissing sound. At such times the river is a lively scene with steamers and sea-bound ships, bluff little tugs, and big looming barges. I had many a chat with the passing sailors, for it was well to begin this at once, seeing that every day afterwards I was to have talk with the river folk in English, French, Dutch, German, or other hotchpotch patois.

For good humour the bargee is not a bad fellow, but he

will beat you at banter. Often they began with, "Holloah, you two!" or "Any room inside?" or "Got your life insured, Gov'nor?" but I smiled and nodded to every one, and every one on the river and lake was friendly to me.

Purfleet looked so pretty that we made a tack or two to reconnoitre, and resolved to stop at its nice hotel, which I beg leave to recommend.

While lolling about in my boat a fly stung my hand; and the arm speedily swelled, until I had to poultice the hand at night and to go to church next day with a sling, which excited a great deal of comment in the village Sunday-school. This was the only occasion on which any insect troubled me on any voyage, though croakers had predicted in rivers and marshes there would be hundreds of wasps, flies, and gnats, not to mention other more intimate companions.

As I entered the quiet little church at Purfleet, a very old gentleman fell down dead at the door. Here was a solemn warning.

The "Cornwall" Reformatory School-ship is moored at Purfleet. Some of the boys came ashore for a walk, neatly clad and very well behaved. The Captain of this interesting vessel received me on board very kindly, and the evening service there was a sight to remember for ever.

About 100 boys sat in rows along the old frigate's main-deck, with the open ports looking on the river, now reddened by a setting sun, and the cool air pleasantly fanning us. The lads chanted the Psalms to the music of a harmonium, played with excellent feeling and good taste, and the Captain read a suitable portion, and then prayer was offered. Let us both work and pray for poor vagrant boys, whose claim on society is great indeed if measured by the wrong it has done them in neglect if not in precept, nay, even in example.

Next morning the canoe was lowered down from the hay-loft, where she had been kept in safety. How many more strange places she has been housed in since!

After taking in supplies at Gravesend, we shoved off into the tide, and lit a cigar, and now I felt we had fairly started. Then there began a strange and charming *freedom* and *novelty* which lasted unbroken to the end of our cruise.

Something like this is felt when you first march off with a knapsack ready to walk to some vague *anywhere*, or when you start alone in a sailing-boat for a long cruise.

But then in walking you are bounded by every sea and river, and in a common sailing-boat you are bounded by every shallow and shore; whereas, here it was in a canoe, which could be paddled or sailed, or hauled, or carried over land or water to Rome, if I liked, or to Hong-Kong.

Up went my sail, and the reaches got wider and the water more salt, but every part of this course was known, for I had once spent a fortnight about the mouth of the Thames in my pretty little sailing boat, the *Kent*, with only a dog, a chart, a compass, and a kettle.

Here comes the steamer *Alexandra*, its high-terraced American decks covered with people, and the crowd gives a fine loud cheer to the Rob Roy for the newspapers had told of our start. Presently the land seemed to fade away at each side in pale distance, and the water was more sea than river, till at the Nore we entered a great shoal of porpoises. Harmless and agile playfellows, I had never been so close to them before, and in a boat so small as to be almost disregarded by them, often so shy and wily. The canoe rocked on the waves, and the porpoises frequently came near enough to be struck by my paddle, but I did not wage war, for a flap of a tail would have soon capsized me.

After a pleasant sail to Southend a storm of heavy rain

had to be met in its teeth by taking to the paddle, until near Shoeburyness, where I was to stop a few days in the camp of the National Artillery Association, which was assembled here for its first Prize shooting.

The Royal Artillery received us Volunteers on this occasion with the greatest kindness, and as they had appropriated the quarters of officers absent on leave for the use of members of the council of the Association, I was soon comfortably ensconced. The camp, however, in a wet field was moist enough; but the fine tall fellows who had come from Yorkshire, Somerset, or Aberdeen to handle the 68-pounders, trudged about in the mud with good humour and thick boots, and sang round the camp-fire in a drizzle of rain, and then pounded away at the target next day, for these were volunteers of the right sort.

As the wind had then risen to a gale it seemed a good opportunity for a thorough trial of the canoe in rough water, but at a place where she would be least injured by being thrown ashore after an upset, and where I might change clothes after a swim.

The buoyancy of the Rob Roy astonished me, and no

less her stability. In the midst of the waves I even managed to rig up the mast and sail, and as we had then no baggage on board and did not mind being perfectly wet through in the experiments, there was nothing left untried, and the confidence then gained for after times was invaluable.

Early next morning we started directly in the teeth of the wind, and paddled against a very heavy sea to Southend, where a nice warm bath was enjoyed while my clothes were getting dried, and then the Rob Roy had its first railway journey along the Southend pier.

It was amusing to see how much interest and curiosity the canoe excited even on the Thames, where all kinds of new and old and wonderful boats may be seen. The reasons for this I never made out. Some wondered to see so small a boat at sea, others had never seen a canoe before, the manner of rowing was new to most, and the sail made many smile. The graceful shape of the boat pleased others, the cedar covering and the jaunty flag, and a good many stared at the captain's uniform, and they stared yet more after they had asked, "Where are you going to?" and were often told, "I really do not know."

From Sheerness to Dover was the route, and the Rob Roy had to be carried on the coals in the engine-tender, with torrents of rain and plenty of hot sparks driven into her by the gale. At last she was formally introduced to a baggage-waggon and ticketed like a portmanteau, the first of a very long series of transits in this way.

The London Chatham and Dover Railway Company took this new kind of "box" as passengers' luggage, so we had nothing to pay, and the steamer to Ostend was equally large-hearted, so I say, "Canoemen, choose this route."

But before crossing to Belgium, we had a day at Dover, where I bought some stuff and had a jib made for the boat by deft and fair fingers, and paddled the Rob Roy on the green waves which toss about off the pier-head most delectably. The same performance was repeated on the top of the swell, tumbling and breaking on the "digue"[1] at Ostend, where, even with little wind, the rollers ran high on a strong ebb tide. Fat bathers wallowed in the shallows, and fair ones were swimming like ducks. All of these, dressed most bizarre, and the babies squalling at each dip, were duly admired; and then we had a quieter run under sail on their wide and straight canal.

With just a little persuasion the railway people consented to put the canoe in the baggage-van, and to charge a franc or two for "extra luggage" to Brussels. Here she was carried on a cart through the town to another station, and in the evening we were at Namur, where the Rob Roy was housed for the night in the landlord's private parlour, resting gracefully upon two chairs.

Two porters carried her through the streets next morning, and we tried to paddle on the Sambre, but very soon turned down stream and smoothly glided to the Meuse.

Glancing water, brilliant sun, a pretty canoe, and a light heart, all your baggage on board, and on a fast current—who would exchange this for any diligence or railway, or steamboat, or horse?

A pleasant stream was enough to satisfy at this early period of the voyage, for the charm of rocks and rapids had not yet been known. It is a good policy, too, that a quiet, easy, respectable sort of river like the Meuse should be taken in the earlier stage of a water tour, when there is novelty enough in being on a river at all. The river-banks one would call tame if seen from shore are altogether new when you open up the vista from the middle of the stream. The picture that is rolled sideways to the common traveller now pours out upon you from the front, ever enlarging from a centre, and in the gentle sway of the current the landscape seems to swell on this side and on that with new things ever advancing to meet you in succession.

How careful I was at the first shallow! getting out and wading as I lowered the boat. A month afterwards we would dash over these with a shove here and a stroke there in answer to a hoarse croak of the stones at the bottom grinding against my keel. And the first barrier—how anxious it made me, to think by what means shall we get over. A man appeared just in time (N.B.—They *always* do), and twopence made him happy for his share of carrying the boat round by land, so I jumped in again as before.

Sailing was easy, too, in a fine, wide river, strong and deep, and with a favouring breeze, and when the little steamer passed I drew alongside and got my penny roll and penny glass of beer through the porthole, while the wondering passengers smiled, chattered, and then looked grave—for was it not indecorous to laugh at an Englishman evidently mad, poor fellow?

The voyage was chequered by innumerable little events, all perfectly different from those one meets on shore, and when we came to the forts at Huy and knew the first day's work was done, the persuasion was complete that quite a new order of sensations had begun.

Next morning the boat was found safe in the coachhouse and the sails still drying on the harness-pegs where we had left them, but the ostler and all his folks were nowhere to be seen. Everybody had gone to join the long funeral procession of a great musician, who lived fifty years at Huy, though we never heard of him before, or of Huy either; yet you see it is in the map at the end of our log.

The pleasure of meandering with a new river is very

peculiar and fascinating. Each few yards brings a novelty, or starts an excitement. A crane jumps up here, a duck flutters there, splash leaps a gleaming trout by your side, the rushing sound of rocks warns you round that corner, or anon you come suddenly upon a millrace. All these, in addition to the scenery and the people and the weather, and the determination that you must get on, over, through, or under every difficulty, and cannot leave your boat in a desolate wold, and ought to arrive at a house before dark, and that your luncheon bag is long since empty; all these, I say, keep the mind awake, which would doze away and snore for 100 miles in a carriage.

It is, as in the voyage of life, that each care and hardship is a very Mentor of living. Out minds would only vegetate if all life were like a straight canal, and we in a boat being towed along it. The afflictions that agitate the soul are as its shallows, rocks, and whirlpools, and the bark that has not been tossed on billows knows not half the sweetness of the harbour of rest.

The river soon got fast and lively, and hour after hour of vigorous work prepared me well for breakfast. Trees seemed to spring up in front and grow tall, but it was only because I came rapidly towards them. Pleasant villages floated as it were to meet me, gently moving. All life got to be a smooth and gliding thing, of dreamy pictures and far-off sounds, without fuss and without dust or anything sudden or loud, till at length the bustle and hammers of Liege came near the Rob Roy—for it was always the objects and not myself that seemed to move. Here I saw a fast steamer, the *Seraing*, propelled by water forced from its sides, and as my boat hopped and bobbed in the steamer's waves we entered a dock together, and the canoe was soon hoisted into a garden for the night.

Gun-barrels are the rage in Liege. Everybody there makes or carries or sells gun-barrels. Even women walk about with twenty stocked rifles on their back, and each rifle, remember, weighs 10 lbs. They sell plenty of fruit in the market, and there are churches well worth a visit here, but gun-barrels, after all, are the prevailing idea of the place.

However, it is not my purpose to describe the towns seen on this tour. I had seen Liege well, years before, and indeed almost every town mentioned in these pages. The charm therefore of this voyage was not in going to strange lands, but in seeing old places in a way so new.

Here at length the Earl of Aberdeen met me, according to our plans arranged long before. He had got a canoe built for the trip, but a foot longer and two inches narrower than the Rob Roy, and, moreover, made of fir instead of strong oak. It was sent from London to Liege, and the "combing" round the edge of the deck was broken in the journey, so we spent some hours at a cabinet-maker's, where it was neatly mended.

Launching our boats unobserved on the river, we soon left Liege in the distance and braved the hot sun.

The pleasant companionship of two travellers, each quite free in his own boat, was very enjoyable. Sometimes we sailed, then paddled a mile or two, or joined to help the boats over a weir, or towed them along as we walked on the bank for a change.[2]

Each of us took whichever side of the river pleased him best, and we talked across long acres of water between, to the evident surprise of sedate folks on the banks, who often could see only one of the strange elocutionists, the other being hidden by bushes or tall sedge. When talking thus aloud had amplified into somewhat uproarious singing, the chorus was far more energetic than harmonious, but then the

Briton is at once the most *outré* and singular when he chooses to be free.

The mid-day beams on a river in August are sure to conquer your fresh energies at last, and so we had to pull up at a village for bread and wine.

The moment I got into my boat again a shrill whining cry in the river attracted by attention, and it came from a poor little boy, who had somehow fallen into the water, and was now making his last faint efforts to cling to a great barge in the stream. Naturally I rushed over to save him and my boat went so fast and so straight that its sharp prow caught the hapless urchin in the rear, and with such appointed reminder too that he screamed and struggled, and so got safely on a barge.

On most of the Belgian, German, and French rivers there are excellent floating baths, an obvious convenience which is sadly wanted in Britain, though we have quite as many bathers as there are abroad.

The floating bath consists of a wooden framework, say 100 feet long, moored in the stream, which runs freely through a set of strong bars and chains and iron network, forming a false bottom, shallow at one end and deeper at the other so that the bather cannot be carried away. Round the side there are bathing boxes and steps, ladders, and spring boards for the various degrees of proficiency. Now we have one in London.

The youths and even the little boys on the Rhine are very good swimmers, and many of them dive well. Sometimes there is a ladies' bath of similar construction, from which a good deal of very lively noise may be heard when the fair bathers are in a talkative mood.

The soldiers at military stations near the rivers are marched down regularly to bathe, and one day we found a large number of young recruits assembled for their general dip.

While some were in the water others were firing at the targets for ball practice. There were three targets, each made of cardboard sheets, fastened upon wooden uprights. A marker safely protected in a ball-proof *mantelet* was placed so close to these targets that he could see all three at once. One man of the firing party opposite each target having fired, his bullet passed through the pasteboard and left a clear round hole in it, while the ball itself was buried in the earth behind, and so could be recovered again, instead of being dashed into fragments as on our iron targets, and then spattered about on all sides, to the great danger of the marker and everybody else.

When three men had thus fired, signals were made by drum, flag, and bugle, and the firing ceased. The marker then came out and pointed to the bullet-mark on each target, and having patched up the holes he returned within his mantelet, and the firing was resumed. This safe method of ball practice is much better than that always until lately used in our own military shooting, and the French could tell us how terribly effective it was as an instruction in cool aim.

As we rounded a point there was a large herd of cattle swimming across the stream in close column, and the Rob Roy went right into the middle of them to observe how they would welcome a stranger. When in my canoe on the Nile I have seen the black oxen swim over the stream at night and morning, reminding one of Pharaoh's dream about the "kine" coming up out of the river, a notion that used to puzzle in boyhood days, but which is by no means incongruous when thus explained. The Bible is a book that bears the fullest blaze of light upon it, for truth looks more true when most clearly seen.

The evening fell sombre long ere we came near the town of Maastricht, in Holland, one of the most strongly fortified places in Europe; that is, of the old fashion, with straight high walls quite impervious to the Armstrong and Whitworth guns—of a century gone by.

But all we knew as we came near it at night was, that the stream was deep and strong, and that no lights appeared. Emerging from trees, the current took us right into the middle of the town, but where were the houses? Had they no windows, no lamps, not even a candle?—no, not a spark!

Two great high walls bounded the river, but not a gate or port could we find, though one of us carefully scanned the right and the other cautiously scraped along the left of this very strange place.

The cause of this was that the commerce and boats all turn into a canal above the old tumble-down fortress, and so the blank brick sides bounded us thus inhospitably. At last we came to a bridge, looming overhead in the blackness, and our arrival there was greeted by some Dutch lads upon it with a shower of stones pattering pitilessly upon the delicate cedar of our canoes.

At last we found a place where we could cling to the wall, which here sloped a little with débris, and now there was nothing for it but to haul the boats up bodily over the impregnable fortification, and thus carry them into the sleepy town. No wonder the *octroi* guard stared as his lamplight fell on two gaunt men in grey, carrying what seemed to him a pair of long coffins, but he was a sensible, though surprised individual, and he guided us well, stamping through the dark deserted streets to an hotel.

Though the canoes in a cart made a decided impression at the railway-station next day, and our arguments logically proved that the boats must go as baggage, the porters were dense to conviction, and obdurate to persuasion, until all at once a sudden change took place; they rushed at us, caught up with two neglected "bateaux," ran with them to the luggage-van, pushed them in, banged the door, piped the whistle, and as the train went off—"Do you know why they have yielded so suddenly?" said a Dutchman, who could speak English. "Not at all," said we. "Because I told them one of you was the son of the Prime Minister, and the other Lord Russell's son."

But a change of railway had to be made at Aix-la-Chappelle, and after a hard struggle we had nearly surrendered the boats to the "merchandise train," to limp along the line at night and to arrive "perhaps tomorrow." The superintendent seemed to clutch the boats as his prize, but as he gloried a little too loudly, his rival in dignity, the "Chef" of the passengers' baggage, came, listened, and with calm mien ordered for us a special covered truck, and on arriving at Cologne there was "nothing to pay."[3]

To be quiet we went to the Belle Vue, at Deutz, which is opposite Cologne, but a great Singing Society had its gala there, and sang and drank prodigiously. Next day (Sunday too) this same quiet Deutz had a "Schutzen Fest," where the man who had hit the target best was dragged about in an open carriage with his wife, both wearing brass crowns, and bowing royally to a screaming crowd, while blue lights glared and rockets shot up in the darkness.

At Cologne, while Lord A. went to take our tickets at the steamer, the boats were put in a handcart, which I shoved from behind as a man pulled it in front. In our way to the river I was assailed by a poor vagrant sort of fellow, who insisted on being employed as a porter, and being enraged at a refusal he actually took up a large stone and ran after the cart in a threatening passion. I could not take my hands from the boats, though in fear that his missile would smash them if he threw it, but I kicked up my legs behind as we trotted along. One of the sentries saw the man's conduct, and soon a policeman brought him to me as a prisoner, but as he trembled now with fear more than before with anger, I declined to give him in charge, though the police pressed this course, saying, "Travellers are sacred here." This incident is mentioned because it was the sole occasion when any discourtesy happened to me during any cruise.

We took the canoes by steamer to a wide part of the Rhine at Bingen. Here the scenery is good, and we spent an active day on the river, sailing in a splendid breeze, landing on islands, scudding about in steamers' waves, and, in fact, enjoying a combination of yacht voyage, picnic, and boat race.

This was a fine long day of pleasure, though in one of the sudden squalls my canoe happened to ground on a bank just at the most critical time, and the bamboo mast broke short. The uncouth and ridiculous appearance of a sail falling overboard is like that of an umbrella turned inside out in a gust of wind. Nobody gets the slightest sympathy for this, or for having the gout or the mumps. I got another stronger mast from a gardener—one of the long, green-painted sticks used as a standard for hollyhocks! This lasted all the voyage, and the broken mast was made into a boom.

Lord Aberdeen went by train to inspect the river Nahe, but reported unfavourably; and I paddled up from its mouth, but the water was very low.

Few arguments were needed to stop me from going against stream anywhere; I have a profound respect for the universal principle of gravitation, and quite allow that in boating it is well to have the earth's strong attraction with you by always going down stream, and so the good rule was to make steam, horse, or man take the canoe against the current, and to let gravity help the canoe to carry me down.

Time pressed for my fellow-paddler to return to England, so we went on to Mayence, and thence by rail to Aschaffenburg on the Main. The canoes again travelled in grand fashion, having a truck to themselves; but instead of the stately philosopher superintendent of Aix-la-Chappelle, who managed this gratuitously, we had a fussy little person to deal with, and to pay accordingly—the only case of good, honest cheating I can recollect during the voyage.

A fellow-passenger in the railway was deeply interested about our tour; and we had spoken of its various details for some time to him before we found that he supposed we were travelling with "two small cannons," mistaking the French word "Canots" for "canons." He had even asked about their length and weight, and had heard with perfect placidity that our "canons" were fifteen feet long, and weighed eighty pounds, and that we took them only for "plaisir," not to sell. Had we carried two pet cameleopards, he would have been just as little astonished.

The guests at the German inn of this long-named town amused us by their respectful curiosity. Our dress in perfect unison, both alike in grey flannel, puzzled them exceedingly; but this sort of perplexity about costume and whence, why and whither is an everyday occurrence for the paddler abroad.

The Main is an easy river, but the scenery is only so so. In a fine breeze upon it we lost much time by forcing the canoes to do yachts' work. Sailing on rivers is rather a mistake unless with a favourable wind. A storm of rain at length made it lunch-time, so we sheltered ourselves in a bleak sort of arbour attached to an inn, where they could give us only sour black bread and raw bacon. Eating this poor cheer in a wet, rustling breeze and pattering rain, half chilled in our macintoshes, was the only time I fared badly, so little of "roughing it" was there in this luxurious tour.

Fine weather came soon again and pleasure—nay, positive sporting; for there were wild ducks quite impudent in their familiarity, and herons wading about with that look of injured innocence they put on when you dare to disturb them. So my friend capped his revolver pistol, and I acted as a pointer dog, stealing along the other side of the river, and "pointing" the game with my paddle.

Vast trouble was taken. Lord A. went ashore, and crawled on the bank a long way to a wily bird, but, though the sportsman had shown himself at Wimbledon to be one of the best shots in the world, it was evidently not easy to shoot a heron with a revolver.

As the darker shades fell, even this rather stupid river became beautiful; and our evening bath was in a quiet pool, with pure yellow sand to rest on if you tired in swimming. At Hanau we stopped for the night.

The wanderings and turnings of the Main next day have really left no impression on my memory, except that we had a pleasant time, and at last came to a large Schloss, where we observed on the river a boat evidently English. While we examined this craft, a man told us it belonged to the Prince of Wales, "and he is looking at you now from the balcony." For this was the Duchess of Cambridge's Schloss at Rumpenheim, and presently a four-in-hand crossed the ferry, and the Prince and Princess of Wales drove in it by the riverside, while we plied a vigorous paddle against the powerful west wind until we reached Frankfort, and dried our wet jackets at the *Russie*, one of the best hotels in Europe.

The Frankfort boatmen were amazed next day to see the two English canoes flitting about so lightly on their river; sometimes skimming the surface with the wind, and despising the contrary stream; then wheeling about, and paddling hither and thither, in shallows where it was "only moist." For fun we both got into my canoe, which bore the weight perfectly well. However, there was not room for both of us to use our paddles comfortably in the same canoe.[4]

On Sunday, the Royal personages came to the English church at Frankfort, and, with that quiet good taste which wins more admiration than any pageantry, they walked from the place of worship like the rest of the hearers.

There is a true grandeur in simplicity when the occasion is one of solemn things.

Next day my active and pleasant companion had to leave me on his return to England. Not satisfied with a fortnight's rifle practice at Wimbledon, where the best prize of the year was won by his skill, he must return to the moors and coverts for more deadly sport; and the calls of more important business besides required his presence at home. He paddled down the Rhine to Cologne, and on the way several times performed the difficult feat of hooking on his canoe to a steamer going at full speed.[5]

Meantime, my boat went along with me by railway to Freyburg, from whence a voyage really new was ready to begin, for as yet the Rob Roy had not paddled in parts unknown.

NOTES

1 At Ostend I found an English gentleman preparing for a voyage on the Danube, for which he was to build a "centre board" boat. Although no doubt a sailing boat could reach the Danube by the Bamberg canal, yet, after four tours on that river from its source as far as Pest, I am convinced that to trust to sailing upon it would entail much tedious delay, useless trouble, and constant anxiety. If the wind is ahead you have all the labour of tacking, and are frequently in slack water near the banks, and often in channels where the only course would be dead to windward. If the wind is aft, the danger of "running" is extreme

A Thousand Miles in the Rob Roy Canoe

where you have to "broach to" and stop suddenly near a shallow or a barrier. With a strong side wind, indeed, you can sail safely, but this must come from north or south and the high banks sadly reduce its effect.

2 Frequent trials afterwards convinced me that towing is only useful if you feel very cramped from sitting. And this constraint is felt less and less as you get accustomed to sit ten or twelve hours at a time. Experience enables you to sit on the floor boards (never take a mat or cushion) with perfect comfort, and on the better rivers you have so frequently to get out that any additional change is quite needless. Towing is slower progress than paddling down stream, even when your arms are tired, though my canoe was so light to tow that I could always draw it by my little finger on a canal.

3 This is an exceptional case, and I wrote from England to thank the officer. It would be unreasonable again to expect any baggage to be thus favored. A canoe is at best a clumsy inconvenience in the luggage-van, and no one can wonder that it is objected to. In France, the railway *fourgons* are shorter than in other countries, and the officials there insisted on treating my canoe as merchandise. The instances given above show what occurred in Belgium and Holland. In Germany little difficulty was made about the boat as luggage. In Switzerland there was no objection raised, for was not I an English traveller? As for the English railway guards, a few of them have the good sense to see that a long light article like a canoe can be readily carried on the top of a passenger carriage, but all the Directors in England do not see that dividends would be increased by a reasonable tariff for canoes, which cause less trouble than ordinary luggage, for the canoeist will always help a porter to handle them. Probably some distinct rules will be instituted by all railways in each country, when they are found to be liable to a nautical incursion; but after all one can very well arrange to walk or see sights now and then, while the boat travels slower by a goods-train.

4 In the Royal Canoe Club we have several "tandem" canoes, each for two paddlers, and they are very fast boats. Each year lately the Club has had races with four men in each canoe, using double paddles. Besides canoes of oak, cedar, or pine, we have them of bark, canvas, tin, paper, and india-rubber.

5 The Earl of Aberdeen was afterwards drowned in a sailing vessel. His brother, the late Hon. James Gordon, was an expert canoeist, and the first to cross the British Channel in a Rob Roy. The present Earl is also a member of the Club, and so was the late Prince Imperial of France, who had four canoes. The Prince of Wales is our Commodore.

CHAPTER III

Höllenthal Pass—Lady Friends—Night Music—Manners—Pontius Pilate—A Schwartzwald Storm—Starers—The Singers—Donaueschingen—Banket—An English Groom—Waiterdom—Source of the Danube—Its Name

Planning your summer tour is a pleasant ploy. It is in June or July that the Foreign Bradshaw suddenly gets interesting, and its well know pages of "Steamers and Railways," and (oh, selfish thought!) only one mind to consult as to whither away.

All this pleasure is a good deal influenced, however, by true answers to these questions. Is this to be a vacation of refreshment, or an idle lounge? Are we going off to rest, or to recruit delicate health, or with vigour to enjoy a summer of active exertion?

But now the infallible Bradshaw could not help me one atom about the canoe, and Baedeker was not written for a boat; so at Freyburg my cogitations ended in the simple resolve, "Go at once to the source of the Danube."

Next morning, therefore, found the Rob Roy in a cart, and the grey-clothed traveller walking beside it on the dusty Höllenthal road. The gay, light-hearted exultation of being strong and well, and on a right errand, and with unknown things to do and places to see and people to meet, who can describe this? How easy it is at such times to be glad, and to think that this is being "thankful!"

After moralizing for a few miles, a carriage full of English people overtook me, and soon we became companions. "The English are so distant, so silent, such *hauteur* and gloomy distrust," forsooth! A false verdict, say I. The ladies carried me off through the very pretty glen, and the canoe on its cart trundled slowly after us behind, through the Höllenthal Pass, which is too seldom visited by travellers, who so often admire the spire of Freyburg from the railway as they pass on their route to Switzerland.

This entrance to the Schwartzwald, or Black Forest, is a woody, rocky, grim defile, with an excellent road and good inns. The villages are of wood, and there is a saw-mill in every other house, giving a busy, wholesome sound, mellowed by the patter of the water-wheel. Farther on, where tourists' scenery stops, it is a grand, dark-coloured ocean of hills. The houses get larger and larger, and fewer and fewer, and nearly every one has a little chapel built alongside, with a wooden saint's image of life-size nailed on the gable end. One night I was in one of these huge domiciles, and when all the servants and ploughboys came in, and half said, half sung, their prayers, in a whining but yet musical tone, and then they attacked a hearty supper.

Our carriage mounted still among crags, that bowed from each side across the narrow gorge, and were crested above by the grand old trees that will be felled and floated down the Rhine on one of those huge rafts you meet at Strasbourg.

But everybody must have seen a Rhine raft, so I need not describe it, with its acres of wood and its street of cabins, and its gay bannerets. A large raft needs 500 men to navigate it, and the timber will sell for 30,000£.

At the top of this pass was the watershed of the first chain of hills, and the Rob Roy was safely housed in the Baar Inn, so I set off for a long walk to find if the tiny stream there would possibly be navigable.

Alone on a hillside in a foreign land, and with an evening sun pouring warm light on the wild mountains, and the playful breeze and the bleating sheep around you—there is a strong sentiment of independent delight that possesses the mind then with buoyant gladness; but how can I explain it in words, unless you have felt this sort of pleasure?

The rivulet was found to be quite unsuited for a canoe; so now let me go to bed in my wooden room, where the washing-basin is oval, and the partitions are so thin that one hears all the noises of the place at midnight. Now the long-drawn snore of the landlord; then the tittle-tattle of the servants not asleep yet—a pussy's plaintive mew, and the scraping of a mouse; the cows breathing in soft slumber; and again, the sharp rattle of a horse's chain.

The elaborate construction of that edifice of housewifery called a "bett" here, and which we are expected to sleep upon, can only be understood when you have to undermine and dismantle it night after night to arrive at a reasonable flat surface on which to recline. First you take off a great fluff bag, at least two feet thick, then a counterpane, and then a brilliant scarlet blanket; next you extract one enormous pillow, another enormous pillow, and a huge wedge-shaped bolster. But why can't the Teutonic race put themselves to sleep at an angle of forty-five degrees, without all this trouble, by merely tilting up the end of a flat bedstead?

Simple but real courtesy followed me throughout. Every one says "Guten Tag;" and, even in a hotel, on getting up from breakfast a guest who has not spoken a word will wish "Guten morgen" as he departs, and perhaps "Bon appetit" to those not satisfied like himself. About eight o'clock the light repast of tea or coffee, bread, butter, and honey begins the day; at noon is "mittagessen," the mid-day meal, leaving all proper excuse for another dining operation in the shape of a supper at seven.

No fine manners here! My driver sat down to dinner with me, and the waiter along with him, smoking a cigar between whiles, as he waited on us both. But all this is just as one sees in Canada and in Norway, and wherever there are mountains, woods, and torrent streams, with a sparse population; and, as in Norway too, you see at once that all can read, and they do read. There is more reading in one day in a common house in Germany than in a month at the same sort of place in France.[1]

I had hired the cart and driver by the day, but he by no means admired my first directions next morning—namely, to take the boat off the main road, so as to get to the Titisee, a pretty mountain lake about four miles long, and surrounded by wooded knolls. His arguments and objections were evidently superficial, for something deeper than he said was in his mind. In fact, it appears that, by a superstition long cherished there, Pontius Pilate is supposed to be in that deep, still lake, and dark rumours were told that he would surely drag me down if I ventured upon it.[2]

Of course, this decided the matter, and when I launched the Rob Roy from the pebbly shore in a fine foggy morning, and in full view of the inhabitants of the region (eight in number at last census), we had a most pleasant paddle for several miles. At a distance the boat was invisible, being so low in the water, and they said that "only a man was seen sitting on the surface, whirling a paddle about his head."

There is nothing remarkable or picturesque about this lake, except that it is 3,000 feet above the sea and very lonely, in the middle of the Black Forest. Certainly no English boat has been there before.

After this, the Rob Roy is carted again still further into the forests. Lumbering vehicles meet us, all carrying wood. Some have joined three carts together and have eight horses. Others have a bullock or two besides, and all the men are intelligent enough, for they stop and stare, and my driver deigns to tell them, in a patois wholly beyond me, as to what a strange fare he had got with a boat and no other luggage. In the end they shake their heads, but invariably conclude that the canoe is being carried about for sale, and, indeed, it could have been well sold frequently already.

About mid-day my sage driver began to mutter something at intervals, with gestures and glances about a storm overhead. The mixture of English, French, and German on the borders of the Rhine accustoms one to hear odd words. "Shall have you pottyto?" says a waiter, and he is asking if you will have potatoes. Another hands you a dish, saying it is "sweetbone," and you must know it is "sweetbread."

Yes, the storm came, and as it seldom does come except in such places. I once heard a thunder-peal while standing on the crater of Vesuvius, and I have seen the bright lightning, in cold and grand beauty, playing on the Falls of Niagara in a sombre night, but the vividness of the flashes today in the Black forest, and the crashing, rolling, and booming of the terrible and majestic battery of heaven was astounding. Once a bolt fell so near and with such a blaze that the horse, albeit tired enough, started off down a hill and made me quite nervous lest he should overturn the cart and injure my precious boat, which naturally was more and more dear to me as she was longer my sole companion.

As we toiled up the Rothenhaus Pass, down came the rain, whistling and rushing through the cold, dark forests of larch, and blackening the top of great Feldberg, the highest mountain here, and then pouring heavy and fast on the cart and horse, the man, the canoe, and myself. This was the last rain my boat got in the tour. All other days I spent in her were perfectly dry.

People stared out of their windows to see a cart and a boat in this heavy shower—what! a boat, up here in the hills? Where can it be going and whose is it? They then ran out to us, and forced the driver to harangue, and he tried to satisfy their curiosity, but his explanation never seemed to be quite exhaustive, for they turned homeward very dubious and looking grave, even though I nodded and laughed to them through the bars of the cart, lifting up my head among the wet straw.

The weather dried up its tears at last, and the hot sun glittered on the road, still sparkling with its rivulets of rain, and the boat was dried by a sponge, and a smart walk warmed its well-soaked captain. The horse too had got into a cheerful vein and actually trotted with excitement, for now it was down hill, and bright sun—a welcome change in ten minutes from our labouring up a steep forest road in a thunder-storm.

The most rigid teetotaller (I am only a temperance man) would probably allow that just a very small glass of kirchwasser might be prescribed at this moment with advantage, and as there was no "faculty" there but myself, I administered the dose medicinally to the driver and to his employer, and gave a bran-mash and a rub down to the horse, which made all three of us better satisfied with ourselves, and each other, and so we jogged on again.

By dusk I marched into Donaueschingen, and on crossing the little bridge saw at once I could begin the Danube from its very source, for there were at least three inches of water in the middle of the stream. In five minutes a crowd assembled round the boat, even before it could be removed from the cart.[3]

The ordinary idlers came first, then the more shy townspeople, and then a number of strange folk, whose exact position I could not make out, until it was explained that the great singing meeting for that part of Germany was to be held next day in the town, and so there were 600 visitors, all men of some means and intelligence, who were collected from a wide country round about. The town was in gala for this meeting of song. The inns were full, but still the good landlord of the "Poste" by the bridge gave me an excellent room, and the canoe was duly borne aloft in procession to the coachhouse. What a din these tenors and basses did make at the table d'hôte! Everything about the Rob Roy had to be told a dozen times over to them, while my driver had a separate lecture-room on the subject for an audience below.

The town was well worth inspection next day, for it was in a violent fit of decoration. Every house was tidied up, and all the streets were swept clean. From the humbler windows hung green boughs and garlands, rugs, quilts, and blankets; while banners, Venetian streamers, arches, mottoes, and wreaths of flowers announced the wealthier houses. Crowds of gaping peasants paraded the streets and jostled against bands drumming and tromboning, and marching in a rickety manner over the rough pavement. Every now and then the bustle had a fresh paroxysm when four horses rattled along, bringing in new visitors from some distant choir. They are coming, you see, in a long four-wheeled cart, covered with evergreens, and bearing four pine trees in it erect among sacks which are used as seats—only the inmates do not sit but stand up in the cart, and shout, and sing, and wave banner aloft, while the hundreds of on-lookers roar out the "Hoch," the German Hurrah! with only one note.

As every window had its ornament or device, I made one for mine also, and my sails were festooned (rather tastefully, I flatter myself) to support the little blue silk English jack of the canoe. This complimentary display was speedily recognized by the Germans, who greeted it with cheers, and sung glees below, and improvised verses about England, and then sang round the boat itself, laughing, shouting, and hurrahing boisterously with the vigour of youthful lungs. Never tell me again that the Germans are phlegmatic!

They had a "banket" in the evening at the Museum. It was "free for all," and so 400 came on these cheap terms, and all drank beer from long glass cylinders at a penny a glass, all smoked cigars at a farthing a piece, and all talked and all sang, though a splendid brass band was playing beside them, and whenever it stopped a glee or chorus commenced.

The whole affair was a scene of bewildering excitement, very curious to contemplate for one sitting in the midst. Next to me I found a young bookseller who had sold me a French book in the morning. He said I must take a ticket for the Sunday concert; but I told him I was an Englishman, and had learned in my country that it was God's will and for man's good to keep Sunday for far better things, which are too much forgotten when one day in seven is not saved from the business, excitement, and giddiness of everyday life. And is there not a feeling of dull sameness about the unmarked flight of time in those countries and places where the week is not steadied and centred round a solid day on which lofty and deep things, pure and lasting things, may have at least some hours of our attention?

So I left the merry singers to bang their drums and hoch! at each other in the great hall provided for their use by the Prince of Furstemburg. He had reared this near his stables, in which are many good horses, some of the best being English, and named on their stalls "Miss", "Pet", "Lady", or "Tom," &c.

An English gentleman whom I met afterwards had been travelling through Germany with a four-in-hand drag, and he came to Donaueschingen, where the Prince soon heard of his arrival. Next day His Serene Highness was at his stables, and seeing an English visitor there, he politely conducted the stranger over the whole establishment, explaining every item with minute care. He found out afterwards that this visitor was not the English gentleman, but only his groom!

The intelligence, activity, and good temper of most of the German waiters in hotels will surely be observed by travellers whose daily enjoyment depends so much on that class. Here, for instance, is a little waiter at the Poste Inn. He is the size of a boy, but looks twenty years older. His face is flat, and broad, and brown, and so is his jacket. His shoulders are high, and he reminds you of those four everlasting German juveniles, with thick comforters about their necks, who stand in London streets, looking diverse ways, blowing brass bombardones, with their cheeks puffed out, and their cold grey eyes turning on all objects while the music, or at any rate a noise, blurts out as if mechanically from the big, unpolished instruments held by their red, numbed fingers.

This waiter lad then is all the day at the beck of all, and never gets a night undisturbed, yet he is as obliging at ten o'clock in the dark as for the early coffee at sunrise, and he quite agrees with each guest in the belief that *his* particular cutlet or cognac is the most important feature of the hour.

I honour this sort of man. He fills a hard place well, and Bismarck or Beaconsfield cannot do more.

Then, again, there is Ulric, the other waiter, hired only for today as an "extra," to meet the crush of hungry vocalists who will soon fill the *saal*. He is timid yet, being young, and only used to a village inn where "The Poste at Donaueschingen" is looked up to with solemn admiration as the pink of fashion. He was learning French too, and was sentimental, so I gave him a very matter-of-fact book, and then he asked me to let him sit in the canoe while I was to paddle it down the river to his home! The naïve simplicity of this request was truly refreshing, and if we had been sure of shallow water all the way, it would have been amusing to carry such a passenger.

The actual source of the Danube is by no means agreed upon any more than the source of the Nile. I had a day's exploration of the country, after seeking exact information on this point from the townspeople in vain. The land round Donaueschingen is a spongy soil, with numerous rivulets and a few large streams. I went along one of these, the Brege, which rises twenty miles away, near St. Martin, and investigated about ten miles of another, the Brigach, a brook rising near St. George, about a mile from the source of the Neckar, which river runs to the Rhine. These streams join near Donaueschingen, but by the town there bubbles up a clear spring of water in the gardens of the Prince near the church, and this, the infant Danube, runs into the other water, already wide enough for a boat, but which then for the first time has the name of the Donau.

The name, it is said, is never given to either of the two larger rivulets, because sometimes both have been known to fail in dry summers, while the bubbling spring has been perennial for ages.

The Brege and another confluent are caused to fill an artificial pond close by the Brigach. This lake is wooded round, and has a pretty island, and swans and gold fish. A waterwheel (in vain covered for concealment) pumps up water to flow from an inverted horn amid a group of statuary in this romantic pond, and the stream flowing it also joins the others, and forms what is now the Danube, the old Roman Ister.

That there might be no mistake however in this matter about the various rivulets, I went up each stream until it would not float a canoe.

The name Donau is pronounced "Doanow." Hilbert says, "Dönau allied to Dón and Düna (a river)." In Celtic *Dune* means "river" and *Don* means "brown," while "*au*" in German is "island" (like the English "eyot").

These rivers are depicted in the plan on our map, and they seem to preserve traces of their Roman names. Thus the "Brigach" is the stream coming from the north, where "Alt Breisach," a name on the bright roll of the war list, now represents the Roman "Mons Brisiacus," while the "Brege" may be referred to "Brigantii," the people about the "Brigantinus Lacus," now the "Boden See" (Lake Constance), where also Bregentz now represents the Roman "Brigantius." The river Neckar was "Nicer" of old, and the Black Forest was "Hercynia Silva." As this log of mine is now honoured by adoption among the reading books of the "London School board," I wish the pupils joy in cracking such nuts as we have here.

The reader also being sufficiently confused about the source of the Danube and its name, let us leave the Latin in the quagmire and jump nimbly into our canoe.

NOTES

1 In 1867 the number of newspapers published in Europe in the German language was 3241, of which 747 were political. In the siege time they printed them even at Versailles.

2 The legend about Pilate extends over Germany and Italy. Even on the flanks of the Stromboli there is a *talus* of the volcano which people dare not approach, "because of Pontius Pilate."

3 After trying various modes of securing the canoe in a springless cart for long journeys on rough and hilly roads, I am convinced that the best way is to fasten two ropes across the top of a long cart, and let the boat lie on these, which will bear it like springs, and so modify the jolts. The painter is then made fast fore and aft, so as to keep the boat from moving back and forward. All plans for using trusses of straw, &c., fail after a few miles of rolling gravel and coarse ruts.

CHAPTER IV

The Danube—"Guten Tag"—Canoe Pleasures—All R-r-r-r-ight—The Weed—Shooting a dam—Day's delights—Toy Barrow—Tuttlingen—The Crowds—The Monastery—Melanie—Tracts—Monks' Cowls—Distance travelled—Reflections

From near the little bridge, on August 28, while the singers *sol-faed* excessively, and shouted "hochs" and farewells to the English "flagge," and the landlord bowed (his bill of thirteen francs for three full days being duly paid), and the populace stared, the Rob Roy shot off like an arrow on a river delightfully new.

At first the Danube is a few feet broad, but it soon enlarges, and the streams of a great plain quickly bring its volume to that of the Thames at Henley. The quiet, dark Donau winds about then in slow serpentine smoothness for hours in a level mead, with waving sedge on the banks and silken sleepy weeds in the water. Here the long-necked, long-winged, long-legged heron, that seems to have forgotten to get a body, flocks by scores with various ducks, while pretty painted butterflies float on the sunbeams, and fierce-looking dragon-flies simmer in the air.

The haymakers are at work; and halt their work hammering the soft edges of their miserable scythes, and they then dip them in the water. Now they have a chat; and as I whiz by the honest group there is a row of open mouths and wondering eyes, but an immediate return to courtesy with a touch of the hat and "Guten Tag," when presence of mind is restored. They call to their mates, and laugh with rustic satisfaction—a laugh that is real and true, not cynical, but the recognition of a strange incongruity, as they gaze on a man pent up in a boat and hundreds of miles from home, yet whistling most cheerfully all the time.

Soon the hills on either side have houses and old castles, and then wood, and lastly, rock; and with these, mingling the bold, the wild, and the sylvan, there begins a grand panorama of river beauties to be unrolled for days and days. Few rivers I have seen surpass this Upper Danube, and I have visited many pretty streams. The wood is so thick, the rocks so quaint and high and varied, the water so clear, and the grass so green. Winding here and turning there, and rushing fast down this reach and paddling slow along that, with each minute a fresh view, the mind is ever on the *qui vive*, or the boat will go bump on a bank, crash on a rock, or plunge into a tree full of gnats and spiders. This is a veritable travelling, where skill and tact are needed to bear you along, and where the exertion of either is rewarded at once. I think, also, it promotes decision of character, for you *must* choose, and that promptly, too, between, say, five channels opened suddenly before you. Three are probably safe, but which of these three is the shortest, deepest, and most practicable? In an instant, if you hesitate, the boat is on a bank; and it is remarkable how speedily the exercise of this resolution matures into habit, but of course only after some rather severe lessons.

It is exciting to direct a camel over the sandy desert when you have lost your fellow-travellers, and to guide a horse in trackless wilds alone; but the pleasure of paddling a canoe down a rapid, high-banked, and unknown river is far more exhilarating than these.

Part of this pleasure flows from the mere sense of rapid motion. In going down a swift reach of the river there is the same sensation about one's midriff that is felt when one goes forward smoothly on a lofty rope swing. Now the first few days on the Danube are upon very fast waters. Between its source and Ulm the descent of the river is about 1,500 feet.[1] This would give 300 feet of fall for each of a five days' journey; and therefore the prospect for the day's voyage is most cheering when you lunch in the morning and know that you will have to descend about as much as the height inside the dome of St. Paul" before you reach a halting for the night.

Another part of the pleasure consists in the satisfaction of overcoming difficulties. When you have followed a channel chosen from several, and, after half-a-mile of it, you see one and another of the rejected channels emerging from its island to join that you are in, there's a natural pride in observing that any other streamlet but the one you had chosen would certainly have been a mistake.

These reflections are by the way; and we have been winding the while through a rich grassy plain till a bridge over the river made it seem quite a civilized spot, and, just as I passed under, one of the green-boughed waggons of jovial singers returning from Donaueschingen drove merrily above. Of course they recognized the canoe, and stopped to give her a hearty cheer, ending with a general chorus made up of the few English words of their vocabulary, "All r-r-r-r-ight Englishmánn!" "All r-r-r-r-ight Englishmánn!"

The coincidence of these noisy but good-humoured people having been assembled in the morning, when the canoe had started from the source of the Danube, caused the news of its adventure to be rapidly carried to all the neighboring towns, so that the Rob Roy was welcomed at once, and the newspapers recorded its progress not only in Germany and France, but in England, and even in Sweden and in America.

At the village of Geisingen it was discovered that the boiler of my engine needed some fuel, or, in plain terms, I must breakfast. The houses of the town were not close to the river, but some workmen were near at hand, and I had to leave the canoe in the centre of the stream moored to a plank, with very strict injunctions (in most distinct English) to an intelligent boy to take charge of her until my return; and then I walked to the principal house, and knocked, entered, asked for breakfast, and sat down, and was speedily supplied with an excellent meal. One after another the people came in to look at the queer stranger who was clad so oddly, and had come—ay, *how* had he come? That was what they argued about in whispers till he paid his bill, and then they followed to see where he would go, and thus was there always a congregation of inquisitive but respectful observers as we started anew.

Off again, though the August sun is hot. But we cannot stop now. The shade will be better enjoyed when resting in the boat under a high rock, or in a cool water cave, or beneath a wooden bridge, or with the longer shadow of a pine-clad cliff.

Often I tried to rest those mid-day hours (for one cannot always work) on shore, in a house, or on a grassy bank; but it was never so pleasant as at full length in the canoe, under a thick-grown oak tree, with a book to read dreamily, and a mild cigar at six for a penny, grown in the fields we had passed, and made up at yesterday's inn.[2]

Let it be well understood that this picture only describes the resting time, and not the active hours of progress in the cooler part of the day before and after the bright meridian sun. In working hours there was no lazy lolling, the enjoyment was that of delightful exertion, varied at every reach of the river.

You start indeed, quietly enough, but are sure soon to hear the well-known rushing sound of a milldam, and this five or six times almost every day. On coming to it I usually went straight along the top of the weir, looking over for a good place to descend by, and surveying the innumerable little streams below to see my best course afterwards. By this time the miller and his family and his men, and all the neighbours would run down to see the new sight, but I always lifted out my little black knapsack and put my paddle on shore, and then stepped out and pulled by boat over or round the obstruction, sometimes through a hayfield or two, or by a lane, or along a wall, and then launched her again in deep water. Dams less than four feet high one can "shoot" with a headlong plunge into the little billows at the foot, but this wrenches the boat if it strikes against a stone, and it is better to get out and ease her through, lift her over, or drag her round.

In other places I had to sit astride on the stern of the canoe, with both legs in the water, fending her off from big stones on either side and cautiously steering.[3]

But with these amusements, and a little wading, you sit quite dry, and, leaning against the backboard, smoothly glide past every danger, lolling at ease where the current is excessive, and where it would not be safe to add impetus, for the shock of a collision there would break the strongest boat.

If incidents like these, and the scenery and the people ashore, were not enough to satisfy the ever greedy mind, some louder plashing, with a deeper roar, would announce the rapids. This sound was sure to waken up any sleepiness, and once in the middle of rough water all had to be energy and life. I never had a positive upset in any voyage, but of course I had to jump out frequently to save the boat, for the first care was the canoe, and the second was my luggage, to keep it all dry, the sketch-book in particular, while the third object was to get on comfortably and fast. After hours of these pleasures of work and rest, and a vast deal seen and heard and felt that would take too long to tell, the waning sun, and the cravings within for dinner, warned me surely that I had come near the stopping-place for the night.

The town of Tuttlingen is built on both sides of the river, and almost every house is a dyer's shop or a tannery, with men beating, scraping and washing hides in the water. As I allowed the boat to drift these boys soon found her out—a new object—and therefore to boys (and may it always be so) well worth a shout and a run; so a whole posse of little Germans scampered along beside me, but I could not see any feasible-looking inn.

It is one of the privileges of this water tour that you can survey calmly all the whereabouts; and being out of reach of the touters and porters who harass the wretched traveller delivered to their grasp from an omnibus or a steamboat, you can philosophize on the whole *morale* of a town, and if so inclined can pass it, and simply go on. In fact, on several occasions when I did not fancy a town, I went on to another. However, we were fairly nonplussed now. It would not do to go further, for it was not a thickly peopled country; but we went nearly to the end of the place in search of a good landing, till we turned into a millrace and stepped ashore.

The crowd pressed so closely that I had to fix on a boy who had a toy barrow with four little wheels, and amid much laughter I persuaded the boy to lend it (of course as a great honour to him), and so we pulled the boat on this to the hotel. The boy's sixpence of reward was a fact that brought all the juvenile population together, and though we hoisted the canoe into a hayloft and gave very positive injunction to the ostler to keep her safe, there was soon a string of older sightseers admitted one by one; and even at night they were mounting the ladder with lanterns, women as well as men, to examine the "schiff."

A total change of garments usually enabled me to stroll through the villages in the evening without being recognized, but here I was instantly known as I emerged for a walk, and it was evident that an unusual attendance must be expected in the morning.

Tuttlingen is a very curious old town, with a good inn and bad pavement, tall houses, all leaning here and there, and big, clumsy, honest-looking men lounging after their

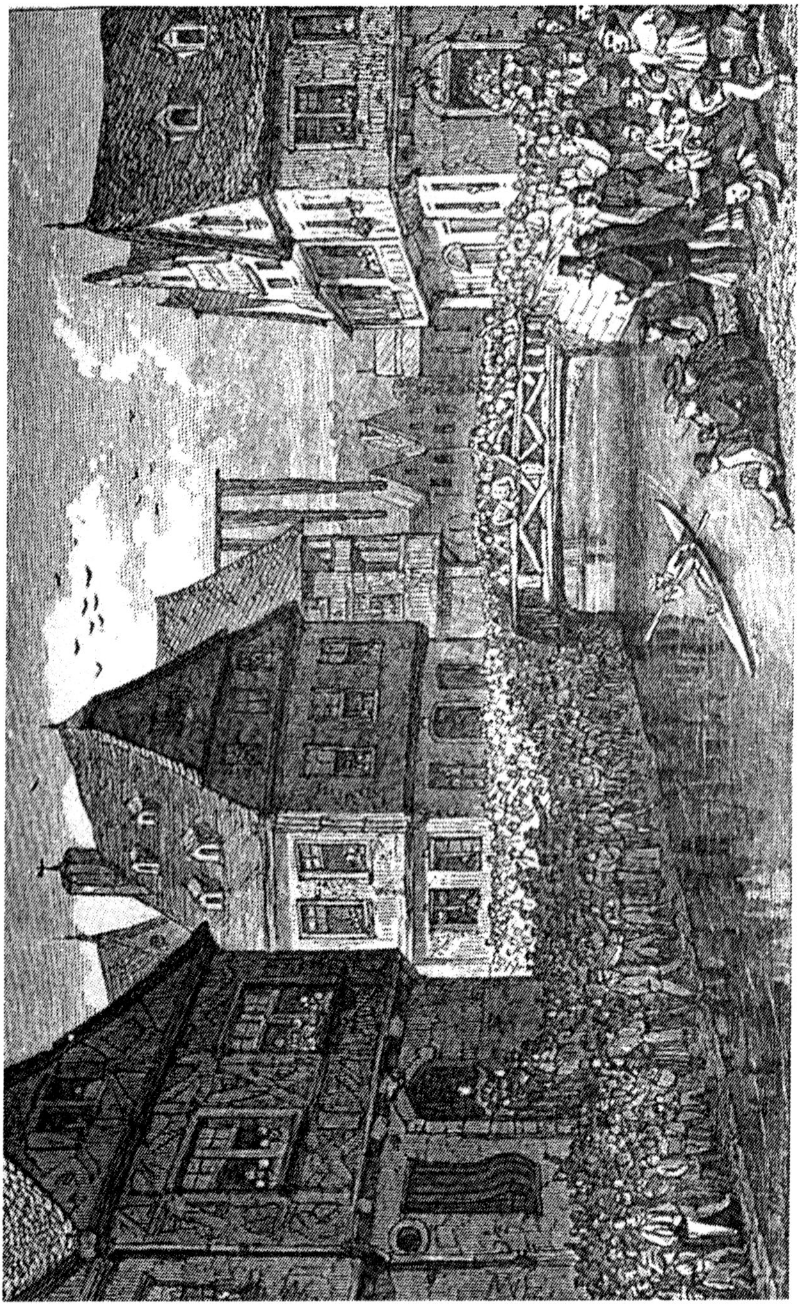

work, and wonderfully satisfied to chat in groups amid the signal darkness of unlighted streets; very fat horses, and pleasant-looking women, a bridge, and numerous schoolboys; these are my impressions of Tuttlingen.

Even at six o'clock next morning these boys had begun to assemble for the sight they expected, and those of them who had satchels on their backs seemed grievously disappointed to find the start would not come off before their hour for early school.

However, the grown-up people came instead, and flocked to the bridge and its approaches. While I was endeavoring to answer all the usual questions as to the boat, a man respectfully asked me to delay the start five minutes, as his aged father, who was bedridden, wished exceedingly to see the canoe. In all such cases it is a pleasure to give pleasure, and to sympathize with the boundless delight of the boys, remembering how as a boy a boat delighted me; and then again, these worthy mother-like, wholesome-faced dames, how could one object to their prying gaze, mingled as it was with friendly smile and genuine interest?

The stream on which we started here was not the main channel of the Danube, but a narrow arm of the river conducted through the town, while the other part fell over the mill-weir. The woodcut shows the scene at starting, and there were crowds as large as this at other towns; but a picture can never repeat the shouts and bustle, or the sound of guns firing and bells ringing, which on more than one occasion celebrated the Rob Roy's morning paddle.

The lovely scenery of this day's voyage often reminded me of that upon the Wye,[4] in its best parts between Ross and Chepstow. There were the white rocks and dark trees, and caverns, crags, and jutting peaks you meet near Tintern; but then the Wye has no islands, and its muddy water at full tide has a worse substitute in muddier banks when the sea has ebbed.

The islands on beauteous Donau were of all sizes and shapes. Some low and flat, and thickly covered with shrubs; others of stalwart rock, stretching up at a sharp angle, under which the glassy water bubbled all fresh and clear.

Almost each minute there was a new scene, and often I backed against the current to hold my post in the best view of some grand picture. Magnificent crags reached high up on both sides, and impenetrable forests rung with echoes from the canoeist's shout in the glee of freedom and hardy exercise.

But scenes and sentiments will not feed the hungry paddler, so we decided to stop at Friedingen, a village on the bank. There was a difficulty now as to where the canoe could be left, for no inn seemed near enough to let me guard her while I breakfasted. At length a mason helped me carry the Rob Roy into a donkey's stable, and a boy volunteered to guide the stranger to the best inn. The first, and the second, and the third he led me to were all beerhouses, where only drink could be had; and as the crowd augmented at every stage, I dismissed the ragged cicerone, and trusted myself instead to the sure leading of that unnamed instinct which guides a hungry man to food. Even the place found at last was soon filled with wondering spectators. A piece of a German and English dictionary from my baggage excited universal attention, and was several times carried outside to those who had not secured reserved seats within.

The magnificent scenery culminated at Beuron, where a great convent on a rich mound of grass is nearly surrounded by the Danube, amid a spacious amphitheatre of magnificent white cliffs perfectly upright, and clad with the heaviest wood.

The place looks so lonely, though fair, that you could scarcely believe that you might stop there for the night, and so I had nearly swept by it again into perfect solitude, but at last pulled up under a tree, and walked through well-ploughed fields to the little hamlet in this sequestered spot.

The field labourers were of course surprised at the apparition of a man in flannel, who must have come out of the river; but the people at the Kloster had already heard of the "schiff," and the Rob Roy was soon mounted on two men's shoulders, and borne in triumph to the excellent hotel. The Prince who founded the monastery is, I believe, himself a monk.

Now tolls the bell for "even song," while my dinner is spread in an arbour looking out on this grand scene, made grander still by dark clouds gathering on the mountains, and a loud and long thunder peal, with torrents of rain.

This deluge of wet came opportunely when I had such good shelter, as it cooled the air; and it would strengthen the stream of the river; so I admired the venerable monks with complacent satisfaction, a feeling never so complete as when you are inside, and you look at people who are out in the rain.

A young girl on a visit to her friends here could talk bad French rapidly, so she was sent to gossip with me as I dined; and then the whole family inspected my sketch-book, a proceeding which happened at least twice every day for many weeks of the voyage. This emboldened me to ask for some music, and we adjourned to a great hall, where a concert was soon in progress with a guitar, a piano, and a violin, all well played; and the Germans are never at a loss for a song.

My young visitor, Melanie, then became the interpreter in a curious conversation with the others, who could speak only German; and our thoughts were turned on some of the nobler things which ought not ever to be long absent from the mind—I mean, what is loved, and feared, enjoyed, and derided, as "religion."

In my very limited baggage I had brought some selected pieces and Scripture anecdotes and other papers in French and German, and these were used on appropriate occasions, and were always well received, often with exceedingly great interest and sincere gratitude.

Some people are shy about giving tracts, or are even afraid of them. But then some people are shy of speaking at all, or even dislike to ride, or skate, or row. One need not laugh at another for this.

The practice of carrying a few printed pages to convey in clear language what one cannot accurately speak in a foreign tongue is surely allowable, to say the least. But I invariably find it to be very useful and interesting to myself and to others; and, as it hurts nobody, and has nothing in it of which to be proud or ashamed, I am not to be laughed out of it now.

The Kloster at Beuron is a favourite place for excursionists from the towns in the neighbourhood, and no doubt some day soon it will be a regular "place to see" for English travellers paddling down the Danube; for it is thus, and only thus, you can approach it with full effect. The moon had come forth as I leaned out of my bedroom window, and it whitened the ample circus of beetling crags, and darkened the trees, while a fainter and redder light glimmered from the monks' chapel as now and then the low tones of midnight chanting reached the ear. Perhaps it is better to wear a monk's cowl than to wear consistently a layman's common coat in the workday throng of life; and it may be better to fast and chant and kneel at shrines than to be temperate and thankful and prayerful in the busy world. But I doubt.

After leaving Beuron, with the firing of guns and the usual pleasant good wishes from the shore, the Danube carried us between two lofty rocks, and down calm reaches for hours. The water was unspeakably clear; you could see right into deep caverns far below. I used to gaze downwards for so long a time at the fish moving about, and to strike at them with my long paddle (never once hitting any), that I forgot the boat was swinging along all the time, till bump she went on a bank, or crash against a rocky isle, or rumbling into some thick trees, when a shower of leaves, spiders, and rubbish wakened up my reverie. Then, warned by the shock, I return to the plain duty of looking ahead, until, perhaps, after an hour's active rushing through narrow "guts," and over little falls, and getting out and hauling the boat down larger ones, my eyes are wandering again, gazing at the peaks overhead, and at the eagles soaring above them, and at the clear blue sky above all; till once more the Rob Roy heels over on a sunken stone, and I have to jump out nimbly to save her from utter destruction. For days together I had my feet bare, and my trousers tucked up, ready to wade at any moment, and perfectly comfortable all the time, for a fiery sun dried everything in a minute.

The physical enjoyment of such a life to one in good health and good spirits, with a good boat and good scenery, is only to be appreciated after experience; for these little reminders that one must not actually *sleep* on a rushing river never resulted in any disaster, and I came safely home from seven such lonely cruises without a cold or a scratch or a hole in the boat, or one single day regretted. May this be so for many a John Bull let loose to "paddle his own canoe."

On some occasions, doubtless, you may have to wish for the end of the day's work, when arms are weary, and the sun is low, and yearnings of the inner man grumbling for dinner, especially when no one can tell how far it is to any house, or whether you can stop there all night if you reach it.[5]

On the rivers where there is no navigation and no towing paths it was impossible to estimate the distances traversed each day, except by the number of hours I was at work, the average speed, the strength of the wind and current, and the number of stoppages for food or rest, or millweirs, waterfalls, or barriers. Thirty miles were reckoned to be a good day's work, and I have sometimes gone forty miles in a day even in rough Swedish lakes; but twenty-five miles were quite enough when the scenery and incidents on the way filled up every moment of time with varied sensations of pleasure.

It will generally be found, we think, that for walking in a pleasant country twenty miles a day are enough for mind and body to be active and observant all the time. But the events that occur in river work are far more frequent and interesting than those on the road, for you have all the circumstances of your boat in addition to what fills the pedestrian's journal, and after a little time your canoe becomes so much a companion (friend, shall I say?) that every turn it takes and every knock and grate on its side is felt as if it were your own. The boat gets to be individualized, and so does the river, till at last there is a pleasant rivalry set up, for it is "man and boat" *versus* the river and all it can place in your way.

After a few tours on the continent your first hour in a railway or diligence may be new and enjoyable, but you soon begin to wish for the end of the road, and then after a short stay in the town at the end you begin to talk (or think) of when you are to leave. Now a feature of the canoe tour is that quiet progress can be enjoyed all the time, because you have personal exertion or engagement for every moment, and your observation of the scenery around is now most minute and interesting, because every bend and slope of it tells at once upon what you have to do. Certainly the pleasure of a day is not to be measured by the number of miles you have gone over. The voyage yesterday, for instance, was one of the very best for enjoyment of scenery, incident, and exercise, yet it was the shortest day we had. The guide book says, "Tuttlingen is twelve miles"—by river, say eighteen—"From Kloster Beuron, where the fine scenery begins. This part of the Danube is not navigable."

NOTES

1 The best geographical books give different estimates of this, some above and others below the amount here stated.

2 Two stimulants well known in England are much used in Germany—tea and tobacco.

(1) The tobacco plant (sometimes styled a weed, because it also grows wild) produces leaves, which are dried and rolled, and then treated with fire, using an appropriate instrument, by which the fumes are inhaled. The effect upon many persons is to soothe; but it impairs the appetite of others. The use is carried to excess in Turkey. The leaves contain a deadly poison.

(2) The tea weed (sometimes styled a plant, because it also grows under cultivation) produces leaves, which are dried and rolled, and then treated with fire, using an appropriate instrument, by which the infusion is imbibed. The effect upon many persons is to cheer; but it impairs the sleep of others. The use is carried to excess in Russia. The leaves contain a deadly poison.

Both these luxuries are cheap and portable, and are daily enjoyed by millions of persons in all climates. Both require care and moderation in their use. Both have advocates and enemies; and it cannot be settled by argument whether the plant or the weed is the more useful or hurtful to mankind.

3 The invention of this method was made here, but its great advantages were more apparent in passing the great rapid of Rheinfelden, as we shall describe further on, with a sketch, and it was afterwards

used on the Jordan.

4 Murray says: "The Meuse has been compared to the Wye; but is even more romantic than the English river." I would rank the Wye as much above the Meuse as below the Danube for romance in scenery.

5 Famine was never felt in the Baltic voyage. Provisions and a cooking apparatus had been added to the stores. One of the four prizes in the first Canoe Club regatta at Thames Ditton, on April 27, 1867, contended for by five canoes in "a chase over land and water," was a beautiful little kitchen, which cooks for two men and weighs 2 lb. It now bears the following inscription: "Designed by the Captain, presented by the Cook, won by the Purser." In the cruises on the Jordan and the Nile, and the Zuyder Zee, I could sleep in my canoe, and carried provisions for four days, but then there were no weirs to haul over, and often no villages to stop at, and always an imperative necessity to be prepared with food and lodging from one's own resources entirely. Moreover, the safest bivouacs in the east were always in the loneliest haunts.

CHAPTER V

Panting Visitors—Hohenzollern—Roman Nose—Herons in Council—
Among the Haymakers—Boating Boy—Winged Music—Arched
Chasms—Hidden Song—Navvies—Different Dangers—A Gale—
Hungry Nap—Chasing a Church—Snags in Darkness—The Vagrant—
Classics—Hotel Bills

The sides of the river were now less precipitous, and the road came within a field or two of the water, so things seemed quite homely for a time.

I had heard a loud jingling sound on this road for at least half an hour, and observed a long cart with two horses trotting fast, and evidently daring to race with the Rob Roy. But at length such earnest signals were made from it that I stopped, and the car at once pulled up, and from it there ran across the field a man breathless and hot, without his hat, and followed by two young ladies, equally hurried. He was a German, resident for a short time in London, and now at home for a month's holiday, and he was prodigal of thanks for my "great courtesy" in having stopped that the ladies might see the canoe which they had followed thus for several miles, having heard of its fame at their village. On another occasion three youths voluntarily ran alongside the boat and panted in the sun, and tumbled over stocks and stones at such a rate, that after a mile of the supererogatory exercise, I asked what it was all about. Excellent villagers! they had taken all this trouble to arrive at a point further down the stream where they knew there was a hard place, and they thought they might help me in passing it.

Such exertions on behalf of a stranger were really most kind, and when I allowed them to give a nominal help (where in reality was easy enough to get on unaided), they were much delighted and more than rewarded, and went back prattling their purest Suabian in a highly satisfied frame of mind.

Many are the bends and currents, but at last we arrived at the town of Sigmaringen. It had certainly an aristocratic air, though there are only 3,000 inhabitants; but then it had a Principality, though the whole population of this was only 52,000. Fancy a parish in London with a Prince all to themselves, and bearing such a fine grand name too—"His royal Serene Highness the Hereditary Prince of Hohenzollern Sigmaringen." But though I have often laughed at this petty kingdom in the geography books, I shall never do so again, for it contains some of the most beautiful river scenery in the world, and there will always be a grim interest in a name that was the spark to light the tinder only too ready for explosion in a deadly war.

There are pretty gardens here, and a handsome Protestant church, also a few good shops, schlosses on the hills, and older castles perched on high rocks in the usual picturesque and uncomfortable places where our ancestors built their nests. The Deutscher Hof is the hotel just opened, and all its inmates are in a flutter when their first English guest marches up to the door with a boat and a great many gazers. The waiter, too, all fresh from a year in London at the Palace

Hotel, Buckingham Gate, how glad he is that his English vocabulary is now in requisition, sitting by me at dinner and talking most sensibly all the time.

The weather still continued superb as we paddled away. Deep green woods dipped their lower branches in the water, but I found that the stream had sometimes a fashion of carrying the boat under these, and it is especially needful to guard against this when a sharp bend with a fast current hurries you into a wooded corner. Indeed, strange as it may seem, there was more danger to the boat from these trees than from rocks or banks, and far more trouble. For when the boat gets under their low branches your paddle is quite powerless, because you cannot lower one end to hold the water without raising the other and so catching it in the trees. Then if you put your head down forward you cannot see, and the boughs are generally as hard as an ordinary skull when the two are in collision. Finally if you lean backwards the twigs scrape your face and catch upon a nose even of ordinary length, and if you take your hand from the paddle to protect the face away goes the paddle into the river. Therefore, although my hat was never knocked off, and my skull was always the hardest, and my paddle was never lost, and my nose was never de-Romanized by the branches, I set it down as a maxim, to keep clear of trees in a stream.

Still it was tempting to go under shady groves when I tried to surprise a flock of herons or a family of wild ducks.

Once we came upon twenty-four herons all together. As my boat advanced silently gliding, it was curious to watch these birds, who had certainly never been disturbed before by any boat in such a place.

They stared eagerly at me and then looked at each other, and evidently took a vote of the assembly as to what all this could mean. If birds' faces can give any expression of their opinions, it is certain that one of these herons was saying then to the others, "Did you ever?" and an indignant sneer was on another's beak that plainly answered, "Such impudence indeed!" while a third added, with a sarcastic chirp, "And a foreigner too!" But, after consultation, they always got up and circled round, flew down stream, and then settled all again together in an adjourned meeting. A few minutes brought me to their new retreat, and so we went on for miles, they always flying down stream, and always assembling, though over and over again disturbed, until at last an amendment on the plan was moved in their Parliament, and they bent their way aside.

A pleasant and favourable breeze springing up, which soon freshened into a gale, my sails were set, and the boat went at her best speed; dashing over rocks and bounding past the haymakers so fast that when one who had caught sight of her had shouted to the rest of his "mates," the sight was departed for ever before they came, and I heard them behind me arguing in excited tones, probably about the ghost.

But it was a shame to be a phantom ship too often, and it was far more amusing to go right into the middle of these people, who knew nothing about the canoe, who had never seen a boat, and never met a foreigner in their lives. Thus, when a waterfall was found too high to "shoot," or a wide barrier made it advisable to take the boat by land, I used to walk straight into the hayfields, pushing the boat point foremost through a hedge, or dragging her steadily over the wet newly mown grass in literal imitation of the American craft which could go "whenever there was a heavy dew." On such occasions the amazement of the untaught clowns was beyond all description. Some even ran away, very often children cried outright, and when the grey stranger looked gravely on the ground as he marched and dragged the boat, and then suddenly stopped in their midst with a laugh and an English harangue, the whole proceeding must have seemed to them at least as strange as it did to me.

The water of the river all at once became here of a pale white colour, and I was mourning that the pretty scenes in the deep below were clouded; but in about thirty miles the pebbles appeared again, and the stream resumed its charming limpid clearness. This matter of dark or black water is of some importance, because when it is clear you can easily estimate after a little experience the general depth, even at some distance, but the shades and hue of the water, while the sunk rocks, big stones, and other particular obstacles are of course more visible then.

Usually I got well enough fed at some village, or at least at a house, but in this lonely part of the river it seemed wise to take provender with me in the boat, and to picnic in some quiet pool, with a shady tree above. One of the very few boats I saw on the river appeared as I was thus engaged, and a little boy was in it. His specimen of naval architecture (no doubt the only one he had ever seen) was an odd contrast to my polished canoe. He had a pole and a shovel; the latter article he used as a paddle, and his boat was of enormous thickness and clumsiness, made of three planks, abundantly clamped with iron. I gave him some bread, and we had a chat; then some butter, and then some cheese. He would not take wine, but he produced a cigar from his wet jacket and also two matches, which he lighted with great skill. We soon got to be friends, as people do who are together alone, and in the same mode of travelling, riding, or sailing, or on camels' backs. So we smiled in sympathy, and I asked him if he could read, and gave him a neat little page prettily printed in German, with a red border. This he read very nicely and was glad to put in his ragged pocket; but he could scarcely part from me, and struggled vainly to urge his tub along with the shovel till we came to a run of dashing waves, and then of course I had to leave him behind, looking and yearning, with a low, murmuring sound, and a sorrowful earnest gaze I shall never forget.

Shoals of large and small fish are in this river, and very few fishermen. I did not see ten men fishing in ten days. But the pretty little Kingfisher does not neglect his proper duties, and ever and anon his round blue back shines in the sun as he hurries away with a note of protest against the stranger who has invaded his preserves. Bees are buzzing while the sun is hot, and when it sinks, out gush the gnats in endless mazes to hop and flit their tangled dance, the creatures of a day—born since the morning, and to die at night.

Before the Danube parted with the rocks that had been on each side for days together, it played some strange pranks among them, and they with it.

Often they rose at each side a hundred feet without a bend, and then behind these were broken cliffs heaved this way and that, or tossed upside down, or as bridges high over chasms.

Here and there a huge splinted tooth-like spire of stone stuck out of the water, leaning at an angle. Sometimes in front there was a veritable upright wall as smooth as if it were chiseled, and entirely cutting off the middle of the stream. In advancing steadily to such a place it was really impossible to determine on which side the stream could by any means find an exit, and once indeed I was persuaded that it must descend below.

In other cases the river, which had splayed out its width to that of the Thames at Hungerford, would suddenly narrow its size to a six-foot passage, and a rush down that with a "whishhh!" The Rob Roy cheerily sped through these, but

I landed to scan the course before attempting the most difficult cuts—Oh, how lonely it was!

A more difficult vagary to cope with was when in a dozen petty streams the water tumbled over as many little cascades, and only one was passable—sometimes not one. The interest of finding these channels, examining, trying, failing, and succeeding, was a continuous delight, and filled up every mile with exciting incidents, till at length the rocks were done.

And now we enter a vast plain, with the stream bending round on itself, and hurrying swiftly on through innumerable islands, eddies, and "snags," or trees uprooted, sticking in the water. At the most critical part of this labyrinth we were going to a tremendous pace, when suddenly we came to the fork in the river. One of the two channels was barred by a tree that would catch the mast, so I instantly turned into the other, when up started a man and shouted impetuously that no boat could pass by *that* course. It was a moment of danger, but I lowered the sails in that moment, took down my mast, and, despite stream and gale, I managed to paddle back to the proper channel. As no man had been seen for hours before, the arrival of this warning note was opportune.

A new amusement was invented today—it was to pitch out my empty wine bottle and to watch its curious bobbings and whirlings as the current carried it along, while I floated near and compared the natural course taken by the bottle with the selected route which intelligence gave to the Rob Roy. Soon the bottle became impersonated, and we were racing together, and then a sympathy began for its well known cork as it plumped down when its bottom struck a stone—for the bottle drew more water than my canoe—and every time it grounded there came a loud and melancholy clink of the glass, and down it went.

The thick bushes near the river skirted it now for miles, and at one place I could see above me, through the upper branches, about twenty haymakers, men and women, who were honestly working away, and therefore had not observed my approach.

I resolved to have a bit of fun here, and therefore closed in to the bank, but still so as to see the industrious group. Then suddenly I began in a very loud voice with—

"Rule, Britannia,
Britannia rules the waves."

Long before I got to the word "slaves" the whole party were like statues, silent and fixed in amazement. Then they looked right, left, before, behind, and upwards in all directions, except, of course, into the river, for why should they look *there?* Nothing had ever come up from the river to disturb their quiet mead. I next whistled a lively air, and then dashing out of my hiding place stood up in my boat, and made a brief (but, we trust, brilliant) speech to them in the best English I could muster, and in a moment afterwards we had vanished from their sight.

A little further on there was some roadmaking in progress, and I pulled up my boat under a tree and walked up to the "barraque," or workman's canteen, and entered among thirty or forty German navvies, who were sitting at their mid-day beer. I ordered a glass and drank their health standing, paid, bowed, and departed, but a general rush ensued to see where on earth this flannel-clad being had come from, and they stood on the bank in a row as I waded, shoved, hauled, paddled, and carried my boat through a troublesome labyrinth of channels and embankments, with which their engineering had begun to spoil the river.

But the bridges one had now more frequently to meet were far worse encroachments of civilization, for most of them were so low that my mast would not pass under without heeling the boat over on one side, so as to make the mast lean down obliquely. In one case of this kind she was very nearly shipwrecked, for the wind was so good that I would not lower the sail, and this and a swift current took us (me and my boat—she is now, you see, installed as a "person") rapidly to the centre arch, when just as we entered I noticed a fierce-looking snag with a sharp point exactly in my course. To swerve to the side would be to strike the wooden pier, but even this would be better (for I might ward off the violence of a blow near my hands) than to run on the snag, which would be certain to cut a hole.

With a heavy thump on the pier the canoe began to capsize, and only by the nearest escape was she saved from foundering. What I thought was a snag turned out to be the point of an iron stake or railing, carelessly thrown into the water from the bridge above.

It may be here remarked that many hidden dangers occur near bridges, for there are wooden or iron bars fixed under water, or rough sharp stones lying about, which, being left there when the bridge was building, are never removed from a river not navigable or used by boats.

Another kind of obstruction is the thin wire rope suspended across the rivers, where a ferry is established by running a flat boat over the stream with cords attached to the wire rope. The rope is black in colour, and therefore is not noticed till you approach it too near to lower the mast, but this sort of danger is easily avoided by the somewhat sharp "lookout" which a week or two on the water makes quite instinctive and habitual.

Perhaps one of the many advantages of a river tour is the increased acuteness of observation which it requires and fosters.

I stopped next at a clumsy sort of town called Riedlingen, where an Englishman is a very rare visitor. The excitement here about the boat became almost ridiculous, and one German, who had been in America and could jabber a little in English, was deputed to ask questions, while the rest heard the answers interpreted. Next morning at eight o'clock at least a thousand people gathered on the bridge and its approaches to see the boat start, and shoals of schoolboys ran in, each with his little knapsack of books.[1]

The scenery after this became of only ordinary interest compared with what I had passed through, but there would have been little spare time to look at it had it been ever so picturesque, for the wind was quite a gale, and right in my favour, and the stream was fast and tortuous with banks, the stream was fast and tortuous with banks, eddies, and innumerable islands and cross channels, so that the navigation occupied all one's energy, especially as it was a point of honour not to haul down the sail in the fair wind.[2]

Mid-day came, and yet I could find no place to breakfast, though the excitement and exertion of thus sailing was really hard work. But still we hurried on, for dark clouds were gathering behind, and thunder and rain seemed very near.

"Ah," said I inwardly, "had I only listened to that worthy dame's entreaties this morning to take good provision for the day!" She had smiled like the best of mothers, and timidly asked to be allowed to touch my watch-chain, "it was so *schön*," so beautiful to see. But, oddly enough, we had taken no solid food on board today, being so impatient to get off when the wind was strong and fair. The rapid pace then brought us to Ehingen, the village I had marked on the map for this night's rest. But now we came there it was found to be *too soon*—I could not stop for the day with such a splendid breeze inviting progress; nor would it do to leave the boat on the bank and go to the village to eat, for it was too far from the river, and so the current and sails must hurry us on as before.

Now and then I asked some gazing agriculturist on the bank where the nearest houses were, but he never could understand that I meant *nearest, and also close to the river*; so the end of every discussion was that he said, "Ja wohl," which means in Yankee tongue, "That's so;" in Scottish, "Hoot, aye;" in Irish, "Troth, an' it is;" and in French, "C'est vrai;" but then none of this helps one bit.

I therefore got first ravenous and then faint, and after mounting the bank to see the turns of the river in advance, I actually fell asleep under a tree. The wind had quite subsided when I awoke, and then quaffed deep draughts of water and paddled on.

The banks were now of yellow mud, and about eight or ten feet high, quite straight up from the water, just like those on the Nile, and several affluent streams ran from the plain to join the river. Often, indeed, I saw a church tower right ahead, and laboured along to get there, but after half a mile the stream would turn sharp round to one side, and still more and more round, and at last the tower once in front was directly behind us. The explanation of this tormenting peculiarity was simply this—that the villages were carefully built *away* from the river bank because it is a bad foundation, and is washed away as new channels are formed by the flood.

When the light began to fail I took a good look at the map, and serpentine bends were marked on it plain enough indeed, but only in one-half of their actual number; and, moreover, I saw that in the forest we had now entered there would be no suitable villages at all. The overhanging trees made a short twilight soon deepen into night; and to add to the interest the snags suddenly became numerous, and some of them waved about in the current, as they do on the Upper Mississippi, when the tenacious mud holds down the roots merely by its weight. All this made it necessary to paddle slowly and with great caution, and to cross always to the slack side of the stream instead of by one's usual course, which, in descending, is to keep with the rapid current.

Sometimes I had to back out of shallows which were invisible in the dark, and often I stopped a long time before a glance of some ripple obscurely told me the probable course. The necessity for this caution will be evident when it is remembered that in case of an upset here *both* sets of clothes would have been wet together, and without any house at hand to dry them.

All at once I heard a bell toll quite near me in the thick wood, and I came to the bank, but it was impossible to get ashore on it, so I passed that place too, and finally made up my mind to sleep in the boat, and soon had all sort of plans in course of devising.

Just then two drops of rain came on my nose, and I resolved at once to stop, for if my clothes got wet before I was snugly in bed in the canoe there would be little comfort all night, without anything solid to eat since morning, and all my cigars already puffed away. As I now cautiously searched for some root projecting from the bank to make fast to, a light appeared straight in front, and I dashed forward with the boat to reach it, and speedily ran her into a strange sort of lake or pond, where the stream ceased, and a noise on the boat's side told of weeds, which proved to be large round leaves on the surface, like those of the Victoria Regia. I drew up the boat on shore, and mounted the high bank through a thicket, carrying my long paddle as a protection against the large dogs which farmhouses sport here, and which might be troublesome to quarrel with in the dark. The house we came to on the top of the precipice had its windows lighted and several people were talking inside, so I knocked loudly, and all was silence. Then I knocked again, and whined out that I was a poor benighted "Englander," and hoped they would let me in, at which melancholy tale they burst out laughing, and so did I! After an argument between us, which was equally intelligible on both sides, a fat farmer cautiously took the light upstairs, and, opening a window, thrust the candle forward, and gazed out upon me standing erect as a true Briton, and with my paddle, too, but in reality a humiliated vagrant, begging for a night's lodging.

After due scrutiny he pulled in his head and his candle, shut the window, and fell to laughing immoderately. At this I was glad, for one seldom finds it difficult to get on with a man who begins in good humour.

Presently the others went up, and I stood their gaze unflinchingly, and, besides, made an eloquent appeal in the vernacular—mine, not theirs, be it clearly understood. Finally, they were satisfied that I was alone, and, though probably mad, yet not quite a match for all of them, so they came down gallantly; but then there was the difficulty of persuading the man to grope down to the river on this dark night that he might carry up a boat.

With some exertion we got it up by a better way, and safely locked it in the cowhouse of another establishment, and there I was made thorough comfortable.

They said they had nothing to eat but kirchwasser, bread, and eggs, and how many would I like? So I said, "To begin with, ten;" and I ate them every one. By this time the priest had come; they often used to send for the *Prester* to do the talk. The large room soon got full, and the sketch-book was passed round, and an india-rubber band made endless merriment for the smaller fry, all in the old routine, the very mention of which it may be tedious to hear of so often, as indeed it was to me to perform.

But then in each case it was *their* first time of going through the performance, and they were so kind and courteous one could not refuse to please such people. The priest was very communicative, and we tried to converse in Latin, for my German was not good enough for him nor his French for me. But we soon agreed that it was a long time since our schoolboy Latin days, though I recollect having had long conversations in Latin with a monk at Nazareth, but there we had ten days together, and so had time to practice.

Thus ended the 1st of September, the only occasion on which I had to rough it at all during the voyage; and even then it may be seen that the very small discomforts resulted from gross want of prudence on my part, and they ended in nothing worse than a hard day's work with its breakfast and dinner merged into a late supper. My bill here was 3s. 6d., and the day before it was 4s. 6d., including always wine and luxuries.

NOTES

1 Knapsack, from "schnap," "sach," provision bag, for "bits and bats," as we should say; haversack is from "hafer," "forage bag." Query—Does this youthful carriage of the knapsack adapt boys for military service, and does it account for the high shoulders of many Germans?

2 In the newspaper accounts of the weather it was stated that at this time a storm swept over Central Europe.

CHAPTER VI

Daydream—Ulm—River Iller—Bismarck's Besom—Fredrickshafen—Lake Constance—Idiots—A Wiseacre—On Rhine again—Goosewinged—Sign speech—Gasthaus—With an Arab—Water bewitched—The Emperor—How to Moor—Grand Duchy again—By the Moon—The Idlers

The threatening rain had not come during the night, and it was a lovely morning next day, like all the rest before and after it; and as we were leaving this place I found it was called Gegglingen1 and was only nine miles from Ulm.

The lofty tower of the Cathedral of this town soon come in view, but I noticed it without any pleasure, for this was to end my week on the Danube; and in my ship's log it was truly entered as a "most pleasant week for scenery, weather, exercise, and adventure."

In a pensive mood, therefore, I landed at a garden, and reclined on a warm mossy bank to have a rest and a daydream, but very soon the loud booming of artillery aroused the hill echoes, and then sharp rattling of infantry firing. The heights around were crested with fringes of blue-coated soldiers and glistening bayonets, amid the soft, round, cotton-like volumes of smoke from the great guns spurting out their flashes of fire long before the sound comes. It was a review of troops that was going on, and a sham attack on a fort surmounting the hill, near the well known battlefield of long years ago at Ulm. If they fought in fury, let them now rest in peace. The shame of Ulm is covered by Metz and Sedan.

Come back, my thoughts, to the river at my feet.

I had been with this river from its infancy, nay, even from its birth in the Schwartzwald. I had followed it right and left, as it seemed to toddle in zigzag turnings like a child; and I had wound with it hither and thither as it roamed away further like free boyhood. Then it grew in size by feeding on the oozy plain, and was still my companion when it got the strength of youth, dashing over the rocks, and bounding through the forests; and I had come at last to feel its powerful stream stronger than my strength, and compelling my respect. And now, at Ulm, I found it a noble river, steady and swift, as if in the flower of age; but its romance was gone. It had boats on it, and navigation, and bridges, and railways, like other great waters; and so I would let it go on alone, tumbling, rushing, swelling, till its broad bosom bears whole fleets at Ofen, and at length as a great water giant it leaps down headlong into the Black Sea.

Having seen Ulm in a former tour, I was in no mood to "go over" the sights again, nor need they be related here, for it is only river travel and lake sailing that we are concerned with; while reference may be made to the Guide-books if you wish to hear this sort of thing:

"Ulm, lat. 97°, and old Cathedral (a) town, on two (§) hills (see Appx.). Pop. 9763; situated †† on the Danube."

At that I stop, and look into the water again.

The river is discoloured here—what is called in Scotland "drumly;" and this seems partly owing to the tributary *Iller*, which rises in the Tyrol, and falls into the Danube, a little way above the town. The Iller has a peculiar air of wild, forlorn, bleakness, with its wide channel half occupied by cold white gravel, and its banks scored and torn, with weird, broken roots, gnarled trees, barkless and fallen, all lying dishevelled; surely in flood times, and of dark wintry nights, a very deluge boils and seethes along there.

Then, at last, there are the barges on the Danube, and very rudimental they are; huge in size, with flat bottoms, and bows and stems cocked up, and a roofed house in the middle of their sprawling length. The German boys must have these models before them when they make the Noah's Arks for English nurseries; and Murray well says of these barges, they are "nothing better than wooden sheds floating in flat trays."

In 1839 a steamer was tried here, but it got on a bank, and the effort was abandoned; so you have to go on to Donauwerth before this mode of travelling is reached, but from thence you can steam down to the Black Sea, and the passage boats below Vienna are very fast and well appointed.

Rafts there are at Ulm, but we suppose the timber of them comes by the Iller, for I did not notice any logs descending the upper part of the Danube. Again, there are the public washhouses in the river, each of them a large floating establishment with overhanging eaves, under which you can see, say fifty women all in a row, half kneeling or leaning over the low bulwarks, and all slapping your best shirts mercilessly.

I made straight over to these ladies, and asked how the Rob Roy could get up so steep a bank, and how far it was to the railway; and so their senior matron kindly got a man and a handcart for the boat, and, as the company of women heard it was from England, they all talked louder and more together, and pounded and smacked the unfortunate linen with additional emphasis.

The bustle at the railway station was only half about the canoe; the other half was for the King of Wurtemburg, who was getting into his special train to go to his palace at Fredrickshafen. Behold me, then, fresh from Gegglingen and snags in the immediate presence of Royalty! But this King was not at all kingly, though decidedly stiff. He was rather amusing, however, sometimes; as when he ordered sentries to salute even empty Royal carriages.

Bismarck's besom has swept him right away.

I got a newspaper here, and had twelve days to overtake of the world's doings while we had roamed in hill, forest, and waves. Yet I had been always asked there to "give the news," and chiefly on two points—the great Eastern, with its electric cable, and a catastrophe on the cruel Swiss glacier, the two being at times vaguely associated as if the breaking of the cable in the one had something to do with the loss of mountaineers in the other. So, while I read, the train bore us southwards to Fredrickshafen, the canoe being charged as baggage three shillings, and patiently submitting to have a label pasted on her pretty brown face.

This lively port, on the north side of the Lake of Constance, has a charming view in front of it well worth stopping to enjoy. It is not fair to treat it as only a half-hour's town, to be seen while you are waiting for the lake steamer to take you across to Switzerland. But now I come to it for a Sunday's rest (if you wish to travel fast and far, rest every Sunday), and, as the hotel faced the station, and the lake faced the hotel, this was the very place to stop in with a canoe.

So we took the boat upstairs into a loft, where the

washerwomen not only gave room for the well worked timbers of the Rob Roy to be safe and still, but kindly mended my sails, and sundry other odds and ends of a wardrobe somewhat disorganized by rough times.

Next day there was service in the Protestant church, a fine building, well filled, and duly guarded by a beadle in bright array. The service began by a woman singing "Comfort ye" from Handel, in exquisite taste and simple style, with a voice that made one forget that this solemn melody is usually sung by a man. Then a large number of school children were ranged in the chancel, round a crucifix, and sang a very beautiful hymn, and next the whole congregation joined in chanting the psalms in unison, with tasteful feeling and devoutness. A young German preacher gave us an eloquent sermon, and then the people were dismissed.

The afternoon was drummed away by two noisy bands, evidently rivals, and each determined to excel the other in loudness, while both combined to persecute the poor visitors who *do* wish for quietness, at any rate once a week. I could scarcely escape from this din in a long walk by the lake, and on coming back found a man bathing by moonlight, while rockets, squibs, and catherine wheels were let off in his boat. Better indeed was it for me to look with entranced eyes on the far off snowy range, now lit up by the full harvest moon, and on the sheen of "each particular star," bright above, and bright again below, in the mirror of the lake.

The Lake of Constance is forty-four miles long, and about nine miles wide. I could not see a ripple there when the Rob Roy was launched at early morn, with my mind, and body, and soul refreshed, and an eager longing to begin the tour of Switzerland once more, but now in so new a fashion. Soon we were far from the shore, and in that middle distance of the lake where all shores seem equally near, and where "the other side" appears never to get any nearer as you go on. Here, in the middle, I rested for a while, and the sensation then was certainly new. Beauty was everywhere around, and there was full freedom to see it. There was no cut-and-dry route to be followed, no road, no track on the water, no hours, no timetable to constrain. I could go right or left by a stroke of the paddle, and I was utterly my own master of whither to steer, and where to stop.

The "pit-a-pat" of a steamer's wheels was the only sound, and that was very distant, and when the boat came near, the passengers cheered the canoe, and smiles of (was it not?) envy told of how pleasant and pretty she looked. After a little wavering in my plans, I settled it was best to go to the Swiss side, and, after coasting by the villages, I selected a little inn in a retired bay, and moored my boat, and ordered breakfast. Here was an old man of eight-six, landlord and waiter in one, a venerable man, and we respect age more while growing older.

He talked with me for five hours while I ate, read, and sketched, and feasted my eyes on mountain views, and answered vaguely to his remarks, said in a sleepy way, and in a hot, quiet basking sun. There are peaceful and almost dreamy hours of rest in this water tour, and they are sweet too after hard toil. It is not all rapids and struggles when you journey with a canoe.

Close to the inn was the idiot asylum, an old castle with poor demented women in it. The little flag of my boat attracted their attention, and all the inmates were allowed to come out and see it, with many smiles of pleasure, and many odd remarks and gestures. Disentangling myself from this strange group, I landed again, and, under a splendid tree, spent an hour or two in carpenter's work (for we had a few tools on board), to repair the boat's damages and to brighten her up a bit for the English eyes we must expect in the next part of the voyage.

Not a wave had energy to rise on the lake in the hot sun. A sheep bell tinkled now and then, but in a tired, listless, and irregular way. A gossamer spider had spun his web from my mast to the tree above, and wagtails hopped near me on the stones, and turned an inquiring little eye to the boat lying half in the water, and its master at rest in the grass.

It was an easy paddle from this to the town of Constance, at the end of the lake. Here a *douanier* made a descent upon me and was inexorable. "You *must* have the boat examined." "Very well, pray examine it." His chief was absent, and I must put the canoe in the Custom-house till tomorrow morning. An hour was wasted in palaver about this, and at first I protested vigorously against such absurdity in "free Switzerland." But Constance is not in Switzerland, it is in the grand Duchy of Baden, and so to keep it "grand" they must do very little things, and at any rate can trouble travellers. At length an obliging native, ashamed of the proceeding, remonstrated with the douanier, and persuaded him at least to search the boat and let it pass.

He took as much time to inspect as if she were a brig of 3400 tons, and, when he came to look at the stern, I gravely pointed to a round hole cut in the partition for this very purpose! Into this hole he peered, while the crowd was hushed in silence, and as he saw nothing but darkness, extremely dark (for nothing else was there), he solemnly pronounced the canoe "free," and she was duly borne to the hotel.

But Constance once had a man in it who was really "grand," John Huss, that noble martyr for the truth. In the council Hall you see the veritable cell in which he was imprisoned some hundreds of years ago, and on a former visit I had seen from the tower, through a telescope, the field where the faggots burned him, and from whence his great soul leaped up to heaven out of the blazing pile.

> "Avenge, O Lord, thy slaughtered saint, whose bones
> Lie scattered on the Alpine mountains cold;
> E'en them who kept thy truth so pure of old
> When all our fathers worshipped stocks and stones."
> *Milton.*

Now we enter the broad Rhine again. The water is deep, and of a faint blue, but clear enough to show what is below. The pebbly bottom seems to roll up towards us from underneath, and village churches appear to spin quietly round on the banks, for the land and its things seem to move, not the water, so glassy its surface steadily flowing.

Here are the fishers again, slowly paying out their fine-spun nets, and there is a target hut built on four piles in the river. The target itself is a great cube of wood, six feet on each side. It is fired at from another hut perched also on posts in the water, and a marker safely placed behind the great block of wood turns it round on a vertical pivot, and so patches up the bullet hole, and signals its position.

The Rhine suddenly narrows soon after leaving the Boden See, or Lake Constance as we call it, but the banks again open out until it is a mile or two in breadth. Here and there are glassy islands, and you may notice, by long stakes stuck on the shallows, which tremble as the water presses them, that the channel for steamers is very roundabout, though the canoe will skim over any part of it comfortably. Behind each islet of tall reeds there is a fishing boat held fast by two poles stuck in the bottom of the river; or it is noiselessly sculled by the boatman, moving to a more lucky pool, with his oar at only one side—rather a novel plan—while he pays out the net with his other hand. Rudely made barges are afloat, and seem to turn round helplessly in the current of the deeper parts, or hoist their great square sails in deeper parts, or hoist their great square sails in the dead calm—perhaps for the appearance, as the sail has two broad bands of dark blue cloth for its centre stripes. But the pointed lateen sail of Geneva is certainly a more graceful rig than the lug, especially when there are two masts, and the white sails swell towards you, goosewinged before a flowing breeze.

The river has probably a very uneven bottom in this part, for the water sometimes rushes round in great whirlpools, and strange overturnings of itself, as if it were boiling from below in exuberant volume with a gushing upwards; and then again it wheels about in a circle with a sweep far around, before it settles to go onward.[2]

On the borders of Switzerland the German and French tongues are both generally known at the hotels, and by the people accustomed to do business with foreigners travelling among them.

But in your course along a river these convenient waiters and polyglot commissionaires are not found in attendance at every village, and it is, therefore, to the bystanders or casual loungers you have to speak.

Frequent intercourse with natives of strange countries, where there is no common language between them and the tourist, will gradually teach him a "sign language" which suits all people alike. By this means, no matter what was the dialect of the place, it was always easy to induce one or two men to aid in carrying the canoe, and the *formula* for this was something in the following style.

I first got the boat on shore, and a crowd of course soon

collected, while I arranged its interior, and sponged out the splashed water, and fastened the apron down. Then, tightening my belt for a walk, I looked round with a smile, and selecting a likely man, would address him in English deliberately as follows—suiting each action to the word, for sign language is made more natural when you speak your own tongue all the time you are acting: "Well now, I think as you have looked on enough and have seen all you want, it's about time to go to an hotel, a *Gasthaus*. Here! you—yes, *you!*—just take that end of the boat up, so—gently, *langsam! langsam!*—all right, yes, under your arm, like this; now march off to the best hotel, *Gasthaus*."

Then the procession naturally formed itself. The most humorous boys of course took precedence, because of services or mischief willing to be performed; and, meanwhile, they gratuitously danced about and under the canoe like Fauns around Silenus. Women stared and waited modestly till the throng had passed. The seniors of the place kept on the safer confines of the movement, where dignity of gait might comport with close observation.

In a case of sign talking like the foregoing you can be helped by one substantive and one adverb; and if you pronounce these clearly, and use them correctly, while all the other expressions are evidently *your* language and not theirs, they will understand it much better than if you try signs in dumb show or say the whole in bad German, which would surely give rise to all possible mistakes of your meaning.

But it is quite another matter when you have forgotten—or have never acquired—the foreign word for the noun you wish to name, though, even then, by well chosen signs, and among an intelligent people, a good deal can be conveyed, as may be shown in the following cases.

Once I was riding along the Algerian coast, on the way

from Carthage, and my guide, a dense Kabyle, was evidently taking me past a place I wished to visit, and which had been duly entered in the list when he was engaged.

I could not make him understand this, for my limited Arabic had been acquired under a different pronunciation in Syria; but one night, it happened that a clever chief had lodged me in a kind of booth, just like the top of a gypsy cart. I explained to him by signs (and talking English) that the muleteer was taking me past the place it was desired to see. Then I tried to pronounce the name of that place, but it was always wrong, or he could not make it out. Maskutayn was the place intended, or "bewitched water," a wonderful volcanic valley, full of boiling streams and little volcanoes of salt.

At length, sitting in the moonlight, signs were tried even for this difficult occasion. I put my chibouque (pipe) under the sand and took water in my hand, and as he looked on intently—for the Arabs love this speaking action—I put water on the fire in the pipe bowl, and blew it up through the sand, talking English all the time. This was done again, and suddenly the black lustrous eyes of the Ishmaelite glistened brighter. He slapped his forehead. He jumped up. You could almost be sure he said "I know it now;" and then he roused the unfortunate muleteer from his snorings to lecture him soundly, and so we were directed next day straight to the very place I wanted.

In a few cases of this international talking it becomes necessary to sketch pictures, which are even better than signs, but not among the Arabs. During a visit to the fair of Nijni Novgorod, in the middle of Russia, I passed many hours in the "Chinese street" there, and found it was very difficult to communicate with Ching Loo, and even signs were useless. But they had some red wax about the tea chests, and there was a white wall beside us, so upon this I put a whole story in large pictures, with an explanatory lecture in English all the time, which proceeding attracted an audience of several scores of Chinamen and Kalmuks and other outlandish people, and the particular group I meant to enlighten seemed perfectly to understand all that was intended.

So if you can work your paddle well, and learn the general sign language, and a little of the pencil tongue, you can go very far in a canoe without being starved or homeless; wandering delighted over a very wide field for the study of character.

To come back, however, from the Volga to the Rhine. The current flows more gently as we enter the Zeller See, or Unter See, a lake which would be called pretty if our taste has not been sated for a while by the snowy range background to the views on Constance. But the Lake of Constance sadly wants islands, while here in the Zeller See are several, one of them rather large. The Emperor of the French had passed two days at his château on this lake, just before we arrived, and of course he would have waited a week had he known that the Rob Roy was coming, for in a canoe, if not in a Cabinet, there is nothing like personal government.[3]

However, as we were too late to breakfast with his Majesty, I pulled in at the village of Steckborn, where an inn is built on the actual edge of the water, a state of things most convenient for the aquatic tourist, and which you find pretty often along this part of the Rhine. In a case of this sort you can tap at the door with your paddle, and order a repast before you debark, so that it is boiling and fizzing, and the table is all ready, while you put things to rights on board, and then tie the boat to the window balcony, or, at any rate, so that it can be seen all the time while you breakfast or dine, and rest, and read, and draw.

Experience has proved to me that very few boys, even of the most mischievous species, will meddle with a boat which is floating, but that very few men, even of the most amiable order, will refrain from pulling it about when the little craft is left on shore.

The landlord was much interested in my sketchbook, so he brought a friend who could speak French, and who had himself constructed a boat of two tin tubes, on which a stage is supported, with a seat and rowlocks, the oddest looking thin in nautical existence. I persuaded him to put this institution into the water, and we started for a cruise; the double-tube metal boat, with its spider-like gear aloft, and the oak canoe, so low and rakish, with its varnished cedar deck, and quivering flag, now racing side by side, each of them a rare sight, but the two together quite unprecedented.[4]

The river here is like parts of the Clyde and the Kyles of Bute, with French villages let in, and an Italian sky overhead. We crossed to a village where a number of Jews live, for I wished to visit their Synagogue; but, lo! this was the

Grand Duchy of Baden again, and a heavily armed sentry, ever watching for insidious foes, found us invading the dominion, so he deployed and formed square to force us to land somewhere else. The man was civil, but his orders were unreasonable, so we merely embarked again and went over to Switzerland, and ran our little fleet into a bramble bush, to hide it while we mounted to an auberge on the hill for a sixpenny bottle of wine.

The pretty Swiss lass in charge said she once knew an Englishman—but "it was a pity they were all so proud." He had sent her a letter in English, which I asked her to let me read for her. It began, "My dear little girl, I love you;" and this did not sound so very proud for a beginning. My new boating friend of the double-tubed craft promised to make her a tin *cafetière*, and so it was evident that he was the tinman of the village, and a most agreeable tinman too.

She came to see us on board, and her father arrived just in time to witness a triangular parting, which must have puzzled him a good deal, Amelia waving farewell to a "proud" Englishman and a nautical whitesmith, who both took leave also of each other, the last sailing away with huge square yards and coloured canvas, and the Rob Roy drifting with the stream in the opposite direction.

"Proud Englishman"—the sound of these words was still in my ears though the speaker was out of sight. Can any nation judge any other as to which of the nations is "proud"— *i.e.*, unduly proud, for there is a proper pride for every people? Some philosopher must come from Uranus to answer this, and he will find it much easier to give his verdict on a first survey of the English, the French, and the Americans, than to give a sharp, clear, and crisp decision after he has dwelt among each people and really known them. but here is his present verdict:

"John Bull is complacent before the picture of his ancient victory in freedom's cause, his prosperous family in every clime, and his hopes of peaceful progress to the end of time.

"Jonathan is rightly proud of his past, that began ten years ago, and which has certainly astounded us all, and he exults in a future vastness that has illimitable room to expand in a prairie sea peopled by sanguine fancy.

"The Frenchman exults in France as a brilliant light, though it is more often a beacon to warn us off than a pharos to show a safe harbour; nay, worse, it is a firework of dangerous sparks and loud explosions, but still he is glad that you *must* look at it, and you cannot but hear its noise, and cannot tell what it will end.

"John looks from a height and is proud; Jonathan looks to a height and is proud; while Monsieur makes all of us look at his capers, and he too is proud as the *enfant terrible* of the world."

Every day for weeks past had been as a picnic to me, but I prolonged this day into night, the air was so balmy and the red sun setting was so soon replaced by the white moon rising, and besides the navigation here had no dangers, and there were villages every few miles. When I had enough of it, cruising here and there by moonlight, we drew up to the town of Stein, but all was now lonely by the waterside. This is to be expected when you arrive late; however, a slap or two on the water with the paddle, and a loud verse of a song, Italian, Dutch, a pibroch, any noise in fact, soon draws the idlers to you, and it is precisely the idlers you want.

One of them readily helped me with the boat to an inn where an excellent landlady greeted the strange guest. From this moment all was bustle there, and it was very much increased by a German visitor who insisted on talking to me in

English, which I am sure I did not understand a bit better than the Germans who came to listen and look on.

NOTES

1 It will be noticed how the termination "ingen" is common here. Thus in our water route we have passed Danaueschingen, Geisingen, Mehringen, Tuttlingen, Friedingen, Sigmaringen, Reidlingen, Ehingen, Dischingen, and Gegglingen, the least and last. In England we have the "ing" in Dorking, Kettering, &c.

2 These maelstroms seem at first to demand extra caution as you approach, but they are harmless enough, for the water is deep, and it only twists the boat round; and you need not mind this except when the sail is up, but have a care *then* that you are not taken aback. In crossing one of these whirlpools at full speed it will be found needless to try to counteract the sudden action on your bow by paddling against it, for it is better to hold on as if there were no interference, and presently the action in the reverse direction puts all quite right.

3 That his late Majesty did not forget the canoe will be seen from the following, which appeared in the "Globe" of April 20 (the Emperor's birthday):

"By an edict, dated April 6, 1866, issued this morning, the Ministre d'Etat institutes a special committee for the organization of a special exhibition, at the Exposition Universelle of 1867, of all objects connected with the arts and industry attached to pleasure boats and river navigation. This measure is thought to display the importance which amateur navigation has assumed during the last few years—to display the honour in which is held this *sport nouveau*, as it is denominated in the report, and to be successful in abolishing the old and absurd prejudices which have so long prevented its development in France. The Emperor, whose fancy for imitating everything English leads him to patronize with alacrity all imitation of English sports in particular, is said to have suggested the present exhibition after reading MacGregor's 'Cruise of the Rob Roy,' which develops many new ideas of the purposes besides mere pleasure to which pleasure boats may be applied, and would be glad to encourage a taste for the exploration of solitary streams and lonely currents amongst the youth of France."

The Baltic Rob Roy canoe was at this Exhibition in Paris, and the

Emperor, having seen her performance on the Seine, forthwith bought a sister ship from Searle, and gave it to the Prince Imperial, who, when he became a member of the Royal Canoe Club, called his canoe the "Rhone," and complied with the good custom of exchanging *cartes* with the Captain.

4 Double boats with paddle-wheels, worked by pedals, are now common in England, but they are stupid things. A double canoe sails well on smooth water, if the inner sides of the two hulls are parallel upright planes.

CHAPTER VII

Fog Picture—Boy Soldiers—Schaffhausen Falls—Eating—Bachelor's Fare—Lake of Zurich—Like a Dog—Crinoline—Spectators—Lake of Zug—Swiss Riflemen—Mist Curtains—Sailing—Fishing Britons—Flogging the Water—Odd Britons—Talk-books—A Suggestion.

In the morning there was a most curious change of air; a dense white fog was all around. Truly it was now to be "sensation rowing;" so we hastened to get off into this milky atmosphere. I have an idea that we passed under a bridge; at least the usual cheers sounded this time as if they were above me, but the mist was as thick as our best November Cheshire-cheese fogs, and quite as interesting. On several occasions I positively could not see the bow of my boat, but only a few feet from my nose. The whole arrangement was so unexpected and entirely novel—paddling on a fast invisible stream—that I had the liveliest emotions of pleasure without seeing anything at all.

But then fancy had free play all the time, and the pictures it drew were vivid and full of colour, and, after all, our impressions of external objects are only pictures, so say the philosophers; and why not then enjoy a tour in a fog, with a good album of pictures making the while in the brain?

Sounds, too, there were, but like those of witches and fairies—though perhaps it was only the cackling of some antique washerwomen on the banks. However, I addressed the unseen company in both prose and poetry, and was full of emphasis, which now and again was increased by my boat running straight into the shore. The clearing away of the fog was one of the most interesting evolutions of nature to be seen. In one sort or other every traveller has enjoyed the quick or gradual tearing up of a fog curtain on mountain or moor, but here it was on a beauteous river.

I wish to describe this process, but I cannot. It was a series of "Turner pictures," with glimpses right and left, and far overhead, of trees, sky, castles, each lightened and shown for a moment, and gauzed over again and completely hidden; while the mind had to imagine all the context of the scenery, and it was sure to be quite wrong when another gleam of sun disclosed what was there in reality. For it cleared away at last, and Father Sol avenged himself by an extra hot ray, for thus interfering with his beams.

The Rhine banks here were sloped steeply; pleasant meadows, vineyards, and woods were mingled with tolerable fairness to all three. But almost any scenery seemed to be good when the genial exercise of the canoe was the medium for enjoying it. Soon afterwards the woods thickened, the mountains rose behind them, the current got faster and faster, the houses, at first dotted on the knolls, were closer and more suburb-like, and then a grand sweep of the stream opened up Schaffhausen to the eye, while a sullen sound on the water warned us of "rapids ahead." Some caution was needed in steering here, but there is no very great difficulty, for steamboats navigate thus far, and of course it is easy for a canoe. But when I glided down to the bridge there was the "Goldenen Schiff" hotel. So one was bound to patronize it, because of its name, and because there was a gigantic picture of a Briton on the adjoining wall. He was in full highland costume, though the peculiar tartan of his kilt showed that there is still one clan we have not yet recognized.

Here began a novel kind of astonishment among the people: for when they asked, "Where have you come from?" and were told, from England, they could not understand how this could be, my course seemed as if we came from Germany.

The short morning's work being soon over, there was all the day for wandering about. Drums and a band presently led me to a corps of little boys in full uniform, about 200 of them, with real guns and with boy officers, most martial to behold, albeit they were munching apples between the words of command, and pulling wry faces at the urchins of eight years old, who strove in vain too take very long steps with very short legs.

They had some skirmishing drill, and used small goats' horns to give the orders instead of bugles. These horns are used on the railways too, and the note is very clear, and may be heard quite well a long way off. Much might be done in our drill at home by something of this sort.

It is a short three miles to the Belle Vue, built above the falls of Schaffhausen, and in full view of that noble scene. These great falls of the Rhine looked much finer than I had recollected them some years before; it is pleasant, but unusual, for one's second visit to such sights to be more striking than the first. At night the river was splendidly illuminated by Bengal lights, and the effect of this on the tossing foam and rich full body of ever-pouring water, made thus a torrent of fire, was a spectacle of magical beauty and grandeur, well seen from the balcony of the hotel, by many travellers from various lands. On one side of me was a Russian, and a Brazilian on the other.

Next day, at the railway station, I put the sharp bow of the Rob Roy in at the window of the "baggages" office, and asked for the "boat's ticket." The clerk did not seem at all surprised, for he knew I was an Englishman, and they know well enough that nothing is too odd, queer, mad, in short, for Englishmen to do. But the porters, guards, and engine drivers made a good deal of talk before the canoe was safely stowed among the trunks in the van; and I now and then visited her there, just for company's sake, and to see that the sharp-cornered, iron-bound boxes of the American tourists had not made holes in her oaken skin. One could not but survey too, with some anxiety, the lumbering casks on the platform, waiting to be rolled in beside the canoe; and the fish baskets, iron bars, crates, and clumsy gear of all sorts, which at every stoppage is tumbled in or roughly shovelled out of the luggage van.

This care and sympathy for a mere boat may be called enthusiasm by those who have not felt the like towards inanimate objects linked to our pleasures or pain by hourly ties of interest; but others will understand how a friendship for the boat was felt more in such a cruise; here strong points were better known as they were more tried but the weak points, too, of the frail traveller became now more apparent, and the eager desire to bring her to England unharmed was increased every day when we had made the homeward turn.

The mere cost of the railway ticket for the boat's carriage to Zurich was two or three shillings—not so much as the expense of taking it between the stations and the hotels. Submitting, then to be borne again on wheels and through tunnels in the good old railway style, we soon arrive among the regular Swiss mountains, and where gather the Swiss tourists, for whom arise the Swiss hotels, those huge establishments founded and managed so as best to fatten on the wandering Englishman, and to give him homœopathic feeding while his purse is bled.

For suffer me again to have a little gossip about *eating*. Yes, it is a mundane subject, and undoubtedly physical; but when the traveller has to move his body and baggage along a route by his own muscles, by climbing or by rowing, or by whipping a mule, it is a matter of high moment to him at least, that fibrine should be easily procurable.

If you wish then, to live well in Switzerland and Germany go to German hotels, and avoid the grand barracks reared on every view point for the English tourists. See how the omnibus, from the train or the steamer, pours down its victims into the landlords' arms. Papa and mamma, and three daughters and a maid; well, of course *they* will be attended to. Here is another timid lady with an alpenstock, a long white pole people get when they arrive in Switzerland, and which they don't know what on earth to do with. Next there will issue from the same vehicle a dozen new-fledged Londoners; and the whole party, men and women, are so demure, so afraid of themselves, that the hotelkeeper does just what he likes with them, every one.

Without a courier, a wife, heavy baggage, or young ladies, I enter too, and dare to order a cutlet and potatoes. After half an hour two chops come and spinach, each just one bite, and cold. I ask for fruit, and some pears are presented that grate on the knife, and with a minute bunch of grapes, good ones let us acknowledge. For this we pay 2s.

Next day, for a contrast, I paddle three miles down the lake, and order, just as before, a cutlet, potatoes, and fruit, but this time at a second-rate German inn. Presently behold two luscious veal cutlets, with splendid potatoes, and famous hot plates; and a fruit basket teeming gracefully with large clusters of magnificent grapes, peaches, pears all gushing with juice, and mellow apples, and rosy plums. For this I pay 1s 6d. The secret is that the Germans won't pay the prices which the English fear to grumble at, and the Germans won't put up with the articles the English fear to reject. Nor may we blame the hotelkeepers for their part in this business. They try to make as much money as they can, and most people who are making money try to do the same.

In the twilight the Rob Roy launched on the Lake of Zurich, so lovely by evening, cool and calm, with its pretty villages painted again on the reflecting water below, and soft voices signing, and slow music floating in the air, as the moon looked down, and the crests of snow were silvered on far-off hills. The canoe was now put up in a boathouse where all seemed to be secure. It was the only time I had found a boathouse for my boat, and the only time when she was badly treated; for, next morning, though the man in charge had appeared to be a solid, honest fellow, I saw at once that the canoe had been sadly tumbled about and filled with water, the seat cast off and floating outside, the covering deranged, the sails untied, and the sacred paddle defiled by clumsy hands. The man who suffered this to be perpetrated will not soon forget the Anglo-German-French set down he received (with a half-franc), and I have never forgotten since to observe the time honoured practice of carrying the canoe invariably into the hotel. Another piece of experience gained here was this, that to send your luggage on by a steamer, intending to regain it at the end on your arrival, adds far less of convenience than it does of anxiety and trouble, seeing that in a canoe tour you can readily take the baggage with you always and everywhere in your boats. Freedom is the paddler's joy.

Much of the charm of next day's paddle on the lake consisted in its perfect independence of all previous arrangements, and in the absence of such thralldom as, "You must be *here* by ten o'clock;" or, "You have to sleep *there* at night." So now, let the wind blow as it likes, I could run before it, and breakfast at this village; or cross to that point to bathe; or row round that bay, and lunch on the other side of the lake, or anywhere else on the shore, or in the boat itself, as it pleased me.

I felt as a dog must feel on his travels who has no luggage and no collar, and has only one coat, which always fits him, and is always getting new.

When quite sated with the water, I fixed on Horgen to stop at for a rest, to the intense delight of all the Horgen boys. How they did jump and caper about the canoe, and scream with the glee of young hearts stirred by a new sight! It was one of the great treats of this voyage to find it gave such hours of pleasure to the juvenile population in each place; and along the vista of my recollection, as I think over the past days of the cruise, many thousand childish faces brimming with happiness range before my eye their chubby or not chubby cheeks.

These young friends were still more joyous when the boat was put into a cart, and the driver got up beside it, and the captain of the canoe began his hot walk behind. A number of their mammas came out to smile on the performance, and some asked to have a passage to England in the boat, to which there was the stock reply, given day by day, "Not much room for the crinoline." Only once was given this rejoinder, that the lady would willingly leave her expansion at home; though on another occasion (and that in France too) they answered, "We poor folks don't wear crinoline."

In every group there were various forms of inquisitiveness about the canoe. First, those who examined it without putting questions; and then those who questioned about it without examining. Some lifted it to feel the weight; others passed their hands along its smooth deck to feel the polished cedar; others looked underneath to see if there was a keel, or bent the rope to feel how flexible it was, or poised the paddle (when I let them), and said, "How light!" and then more critical inquirers measured the boat's dimensions, tapped its sides with their knuckles, and looked wise; sketched its form, scrutinized its copper nails, or gently touched the silken flag, with its hem now frayed a little, and its colour fading; in all places this last item (our burgee), as an object of interest, was always the first exclaimed about by the lady portion of the crowd. It is with such light but pleasant trivialities that a traveller's day may be filled in this enchanting atmosphere, where simply to exist, to breathe, to gaze, and to listen, are enough to pass the sunny hours, if not to engage the nobler powers of the mind.

The Lakes of Zurich and Zug are not far separate. About three hours of steady road walking takes you from one to the other, over a high neck of forest land, and a hot walk—this was from twelve to three o'clock in the brightest hours of the day. The heat and the dust made me eager again to be afloat. By the map, indeed, it seemed as if one could row part of this way on a river which runs into Zug, but maps are no guidance as to the fitness of streams for a boat. They make a black line wriggling about on the paper do for all rivers alike, and this tells you nothing as to the depth or force of the current, nor can the drivers or innkeepers tell you much more, since they have no particular reason for observing how a river comports itself; their business is on the road.

The driver was proud of his unusual fare, a boat with an English flag, and he gave a short account of it to every friend he met; an account no doubt frightfully exaggerated, but always accepted as sufficient by the gratified listener. The worthy carter, however, was quite annoyed that I stopped him outside the town of Zug (paying thirteen francs for the cart), for I wished to get the canoe into the water unobserved, as the morning's work had left me yet no rest, and sweet repose could best be had by floating in my boat. However, there was no evading the townspeople's desire to see "the schiff in a cart from England." We took her behind a clump of stones, but they climbed upon the stones and stood. I sat down in a moody silence, but they sat down too in respectful patience. I tried then another plan, turned the canoe bottom upward, and began lining a seam of the planks with red putty. They looked on till it was done, and I began the same seam again, and told them that all the other seams must be thus lined. This, at last, was too much for some of the wiser ones, who turned away and murmured at my slowness, but others at once took their places in the front row. It seemed unfriendly to go on thus any longer, and as it was cooler now, I pushed the boat into the lake, shipped my luggage on board, and after the usual English speech to them from the water, bid every one "adieu."[1]

New vigour came when once the paddle was grasped again, and the soft yielding water and gentle heaving on its bosom gave fresh pleasure now after the dusty road. It seems as if one must be forever spoiled for land travel by this smooth liquid journeying.

Zug is a little lake, and the mountains are over it only at one end, but then there are glorious hills, the Rigi and a hundred more, each behind another, or raising a peak in the gaps between. I must resolutely abstain from describing these here. The sight of them is well known to the traveller. The painted pictures of them in every shop window are faithful enough for those who have not been nearer, and words can tell very little to others of what is seen and felt when you fill the delighted eye by looking on the snowy range.

Near one end of the lake I visited the line of targets where the Switzers were popping away their little bullets at their short ranges, with all sort of gimcrack instruments to aid them, lenses, crooks, and straps for the arms, hair triggers, and everything done under cover too. Very skillful indeed are they in the use of these contrivances; but the weapons look like toy guns after all, and are only one step removed from the crossbows you see in Belgium and France, where men meet to shoot at stuffed cockrobins fixed on a pole, and do not hit them, and then adjourn for beer.

The Swiss are good shots and brave men, and woe be to their invaders. Still, in this matter of rifle shooting their *dilettanti* practice through a window, at the short range of 200 yards, seems really childish when compared with that of the manly groups at Wimbledon, where, on the open heath, in sun or drifting hail, the burly Yorkshireman meets with the hardy Scot, and sends his heavier deadly bullet on its swift errand right away for a thousand yards in a storm.

Leaving the shooters to their bull's-eyes, I paddled in front of the town to scan the hotels, and to judge of the best by appearances. Out came the boats of Zug to examine the floating stranger. They went round and round, in a criticizing mood, just as local dogs strut slowly in circles about a new-come cur who is not known to their street, and besides is of ambiguous breed. These boats were all larger than mine, and most of them were brighter with plenty of paint, and universally they were encumbered with most awkward oars. A courteous Frenchman in one of the boats told me all the Zug news in a breath, besides asking numerous questions, and giving a hasty commentary on the fishing in the lake. Finally, he pointed out the best hotel, and so the naval squadron advanced to the pier, led by the canoe. A gracious landlady here put my boat safe in the hotel coachhouse, and offered to give me the key of the padlock, to make sure. In the *salle à manger* were some English friends from London, so now I felt that here was an end of lone wanderings among foreigners, for the summer stream of tourists from England was encountered at this point.

An early start next morning found the mists on the mountains, but they were quickly furled up out of the way in airy festoons like muslin curtains. We skirted the pretty villas on the verge of the lake, and hauled in by some apple trees to rig up the sails. This could be done more easily when the boat was drawn ashore than when it was afloat; though, after practice, I could not only set the mast and hoist the sails "at sea," but could even stand up and change my coat or tie the flag on the masthead, or survey a difficult channel while the boat was rocking on the waves of a rapid.[2]

Sailing on a lake in Switzerland is a full reward for carrying your mast and sails unused for many a long mile. Sometimes, indeed, the sails seemed to be after all an encumbrance, but this was when they were not available. Every time they came into use again the satisfaction of having brought them was fully reassured. In sailing while the wind is light you need not always sit, as must be done for paddling. Wafted by the breeze you can now recline, lie down, or lie up, put your legs anyhow and anywhere, in the water if you like, and the peak of the sail is a shade between the sun and your eyes, while the ripples seem to tinkle cheerfully against the bow, and the wavelets seethe by smoothly near the stern. When you are under sail the hill tops look higher than before, for now you see how far they are above your "lofty" masthead, and the black rocks on the shore look blacker when seen in contrast with a sail like cream.[3]

After a cruise that left nothing more to see of the Zug, we put into port at Imyn, and though it is a little place, only a few houses, the boys there were as troublesome as gnats buzzing about; so the canoe had to be locked in the stable out of sight.

Three Britons were waiting here for the steamer. They had come to fish in Switzerland. Now fishing and shooting and travelling kill each other, so far as my experience goes, unless one of them is used as a *passetemps* because you cannot go on with the other. Thus I recollect once at the town of Vossevangen, in Norway, when we had to wait some hours for horses, it was capital fun to catch three trout with a pin for a hook fastened on the lash of a gig whip, while a fellow traveller shot with a pistol at my Glengarry cap on a stone.

The true fisherman fishes for the fishing, not for the fishes. He himself is pleased even if he catches nothing, though he is more pleased to bring back a full basket, for that will justify him to his friends. Now when you stop your travelling that you may angle, if you catch nothing you grudge the day spent, and keep thinking how much you might have seen in a day on the road. On the other hand, if you do happen to catch a fish, you don't like to leave the place where more might be taken, and your first ten miles after departure from it is a stage of reflection about pools, stones, bites, and rises, instead of what is going on all around. Worst of all, if you have hooked a fish and lost him, it is a sad confession of defeat then to give up the sport and moodily resume the tour.[4]

As for the three visitors at Imyn, they had just twenty minutes sure, so they breakfasted in five minutes, and in the next three minutes had got their rods ready, and were out in the garden casting as fast as possible, and flogging the water as if the fish also ought to be in a hurry to get taken. The hot sun blazed upon the bald head of one of these excited anglers, for he had not time to put on his hat. The other had got his line entangled in a bush, and of course was *hors de combat*. The third was a sort of light skirmisher, rushing about with advice, and pointing out shoals of minnows everywhere else but where his companions were engaged. However, they managed to capture a few monsters of the deep, that is to say, a couple of misguided gudgeons, probably dissipated members of their tribe, and late risers, who had missed their proper breakfasts. The most ardent Izaak

Walton of us all could not surely enjoy fishing after this sort.

To be in this tide of wandering Britons, and yet to look at them and listen to them as if you were distinct—this is a post full of interest and amusement; and if you can, even for one day, try to be (at least in thought) a Swiss resident or a Parisian, and so to regard the English around you from the point they are seen from by the foreigners whom they visit, the examination becomes far more curious. But this has been done by many clever tourists, who have written their notes with more or less humour, and with severity rather more than less; so I shall not attempt to analyze the strange atoms of the flood from our islands which overflow the Continent every year. It is the fashion to decry three-fifths of this motley company as "snobs," "spendthrifts," or "greenhorns." But is not much of the hard criticism published by travellers against their fellows only a crooked way of saying that the writer in each case has at any rate met some travellers inferior to himself?

Of course, among the Englishmen whom I met now and then in the course of this voyage there were some very strange specimens, and their remarks were odd enough, when alluding to the canoe. One said, for example, "Don't you think it would have been more commodious to have had an attendant with you to look after your luggage and things?" The most obvious answer to this was probably that which I gave, "Not for me, if he was to be in the boat; and not for him, if he had to run on the bank." Another Englishman (but he was at home) asked me in all seriousness about the canoe voyage, "Was it not a great waste of time?" And when I inquired how *he* had spent his vacation, he said, "Oh, I was all the time *at Brighton.*"

In returning again to conversation in English, one is reminded how very unpractical are all the "Talk-books" published to facilitate the traveller's conversation in foreign languages. Whether they are meant to help you in French, German, Italian, or Spanish, these little books, with their well known double columns of words and phrases, and their "Polite Letter writer" at the end, all seem to be equally determined to force words upon you which you never will need to use; while the things you are always wanting to say in the new tongue are either carefully buried among colloquies on botany or precious stones, or among philosophical discussions about metaphysics, or else the desirable phrases are not in the book at all.

This need of a brief and good "Talk-book" struck me particularly when I had carefully marked in my German one all the pages which would never be required in the tour, so that I could cut them out as an unnecessary addition to the weight of my ship's library. Why, the little book, when thus expurgated, got so lamentably thin that the few pages left of it, as just possible to be useful, formed only a wretched skeleton of the original volume.

Another fault of these books is that half of the matter in them is made up of what the imaginary chatting foreigner says *to you*, the unhappy Englishman, and this often in long phrases or even in set speeches. But when, in actual life, the real foreigner does speak to you, he somehow says quite a different set of words from any particular phrases you see in the book, and you cannot make out his meaning, because it does not correspond to anything you have learned.

It is evident that a dictionary is required to get at the English meaning of what is said to you by another; while a talk-book will suffice for what you wish to say to him; because you can select in it and compose from it before you utter any particular phrase. The Danish phrase book for Norway and Sweden is a tolerably good one, and it holds in a short compass all the traveller wants; but I think a book of this kind for each of the other principal languages might well be constructed on the following basis.

First, let us have the expression "I want," and then the English substantives most used in travel talk, arranged in alphabetical order, and with their foreign equivalents. Next put the request "Will you," and after it place each of the verbs of action generally required by travellers. Then set forth the question, "Does the," with a column of events formed by a noun, verb, and preposition in each, such as "coach stop at," "road lead to," "steamer start from," &c.; and lastly, give us the comprehensive "Is it," with an alphabetical list of adjectives likely to be employed. Under these four heads, with two pages of adverbs and numerals, I think that the primary communications with a foreigner can be comprised; and as for conversations with him on special subjects, such a politics, or art, or scenery, these are practically not likely to be attempted unless you learn his language, and not merely some of the most necessary words; but this study of language is not the purpose for which you get a talk-book.

Having talked our homily on international talking, it is time to be on the move again.

NOTES
1 This word, like other French words, is commonly used in Germany and Switzerland.

2 This standing up drill is so very useful in extending the horizon of view, and in enabling you to examine a whole ledge of sunken rocks at once, that it is well worth the trouble of a week or two's practice.

3 The sails of the Jordan Rob Roy were dyed dark blue—an excellent plan for alleviating the glare of an African sun, and for eluding the gaze of hostile Arabs. For an opposite purpose, in lonely Eastern parts, when it was desirable to be discerned afar off by my dragoman, I wore

a bright red jersey.

4 Fishing from a canoe is, however, very pleasant when the current bears you along, as is told in the log of our Swedish tour. One summer, with a faithful mate, my little terrier "Rob," the Rob Roy plunged into the breakers among the seals at the Scilly Isles and round the bold capes of the Cornish coast, visiting 100 German vessels kept in various ports by fear of the looming French warships outside, and then for the winter the canoe was hauled up through a window to her bedroom in the Temple.

CHAPTER VIII

Lake of Lucerne—Seeburg Hotel—Bonâ-fide Bite—The Rapid Reuss—Fair Friends—Is it right?—Caught by a Rope—Barriers—The Hard Place—Din—Headlong—The Struggle—Bremgarten

When the steamer at Imyn had embarked the three sportsmen, and the little pier was quiet, we got a cart out for the Rob Roy, and bargained to have it rumbled over the hill to the Lake of Lucerne for the sum of five francs—it is only half an hour's walk. The landlord himself came as driver, for he was fully interested about the canoe, and he did not omit to let people know his sentiments on the subject all along the way, but call out even to the men plucking fruit in the apple trees, who had perhaps failed to notice the wonderful phenomenon which was passing on the road beneath. There was a permanent joke on such occasions, and, oddly enough, it was used by the drivers in Germany as well as in Switzerland, and was of course original and spontaneous with each of them as they called out, "Going to America!" and then chuckled at the brilliant remark.

The village we came to on Lucerne was the well-known Kussnacht, that is, *one* of the well-known Kussnachts, for there are plenty of these honeymoon towns in Central Europe. In the midst of the customary assembly of *quidnuncs*, eloquently addressed this time by the landlord-driver, the canoe was launched on another lake, perhaps the prettiest lake in the world.

Like other people, and at other times, I had traversed this beautiful water of the Four Cantons, but those only who have seen it well by steamer and by walking, so as to know how it juts in and winds round in intricate geography, can imagine how much better you may follow and grasp its beauties by searching them out with a canoe.

For thus I could penetrate all the wooded nooks, and dwell on each viewpoint, and visit the rocky islets, and wait long, longer—as long as I pleased before some lofty berg, while the groundswell gently undulated, and the passing cloud shaded the hill with grey, and the red flag of a steamer fluttered in a distant sunbeam, and the plash of a barge's oar broke on the boatman's song; everything around changing just a little, and the stream of inward thought and admiration changing too as it flowed, but all the time, whenever the eye came back to it again, there was always the grand mountain still the same,

"Like Teneriffe or Atlas unremoved."

How cool the snow looked up there aloft even in the heat of summer! and—to come again to one's level on the water—how lively the steamer was with the music of its band and the quick beat of its wheels curling up white foam. Let us speed to meet it and to get a tossing in the swell, while Jones and Smith, under the awning, cry out, "Why, to be sure, that's the Rob Roy canoe," and Mrs. Jones and the three Miss Smiths all lift up their heads from their "Murrays," where they have been diligently reading the history of Switzerland from A.D. 1682, and then the description in words of all the scenery around, although they have suffered its speaking realities in mountain, wood, and lake to pass before their very eyes unnoticed.

As I was quite fresh in good "training" now, so as to get on very comfortably with ten or twelve hours' rowing in a day, I spent it all in seeing this inexhaustible Lake of Lucerne, and yet felt that at least a dozen new pictures had been left unseen in this rich and lavish volume of the book of nature. But as that book had no page in it about quarters for the night, it was time at last to consider these homely affairs, and to look out for an hotel; not one of the big barracks for Englishmen spoken of before, but some quiet place where one could stop for Sunday. Coming suddenly then round a shady point, behold the very place! But can it be an hotel? Yes, there is the name, "Seeburg." Is it quiet? Observe the shady walks. Bathing? Why, there is a bath in the lake at the end of the garden. Fishing? At least four rods are stretched over the reeds by hopeful hands, and with earnest looks behind, watching breathlessly for the faintest nibble.

Let us run boldly in. Ten minutes, and the boat is safely in a shed, and its captain well housed in an excellent room; and, having ordered dinner, it was delicious to jump into the lake for a swim, all hot with the hot day's work, and to stretch away out to the deep, and circle round and round in these limpid waters, with a nice little bath room to come back to, and fresh dry clothes to put on. In the evening we had very pretty English music, a family party improvised in an hour, and broken up for a moonlight walk, while, all this time (one fancied), in the big hotel of the town the guests were in stiff *coteries*, or each set had retired to its sitting room, and lamented how unsociable everybody had become.

I never was more comfortable than here, with a few

English families "en pension," luxuriating for the sum of six francs per day, and an old Russian General, most warlike and courteous, who would chat with you by the hour on the seat under the shady chestnut, and smiled at the four persevering fishermen whose bag consisted, I believe, of three nibbles, one of them allowed on all hands to have been *bonâ fide*.

Then on Sunday we went to Lucerne, to church, where a large congregation listened to a very good sermon from the well known Secretary of the Society for Colonial and Continental Churches. At least every traveller, if not every home-stayed Englishman, ought to support this Association, because it many times supplies just that food and rest which the soul needs so much on a Sunday abroad, when the pleasures of foreign travel are apt to make us think and act as if only the mind and body constitute the man.

I determined to paddle from Lucerne by the river Reuss, which flows out of the lake and through the town. The river is one of four—the Rhine, Rhone, Reuss, and Ticino, which all rise near together in the neighbourhood of the St. Gothard; and yet, while one flows into the German ocean, another falls into the Mediterranean, both having first made between them nearly the compass of Switzerland. The walking tourist comes often upon the rapid Reuss as it staggers and tumbles among the Swiss mountains. To me it had a special interest, for I once ascended the Galenhorn over the glaciers it starts from, and with only a useless guide, who lost his head and then lost his way, and then lost his temper and began to cry. We groped about in a fog until snow began to fall, and the snowstorm lasted for six hours—a weary time spent by us hapless ones wandering in the dark and without food. At length we were discovered by some people sent out with lights to search for the benighted pleasure-seeker.

The Reuss has many cascades and torrent gorges as it runs among the shattered crags, and it falls nearly 6000 feet before it reaches the Lake of Lucerne, this lake itself being still 1400 feet above the sea.

A gradual current towards the end of the lake entices you under the bridge where the river starts again on its course, at first gently enough, and as if it never could get fierce and hoarse voiced when it has taken you miles away into the woods and can deal with you all alone. The map showed the Reuss flowing into the Aar, but I could learn nothing more about either of these rivers, except that an intelligent man said, "The Reuss is a mere torrent," while another recounted how a man some years ago went on the Aar in a boat, and was taken up by the police and punished for thus perilling his life. Deducting from these statements the usual 50 percent for exaggeration, everything appeared satisfactory, so I yielded my boat to the current, and, at parting, waved my yellow paddle to certain fair English friends who had honoured me with their smiles, and who were now assembled on the bridge. After this a few judicious strokes took the Rob Roy through the town and past the pleasant environs, and we were now again in happy sport on running water.

The current, after a quiet beginning, soon put on a sort of "business air," as if it did not mean to dally, and rapidly got into quick time, threading a devious course among the woods, hayfields, and vineyards, and it seemed not to murmur as streams generally do, but to sing with buoyant exhilaration in the fresh brightness of the morn. It certainly was a change, from the sluggish feeling of dead water in the lakes to the lively tremulous thrilling of a rapid river like the Reuss, which, in many places, is as wide as the Rhine at Schaffhausen. It is a wild stream, too fast for navigation, and therefore the villages are not built on the banks, and there are no boats, and the lonely, pathless, forest-covered banks are sometimes bleak enough when seen from the water.

For some miles it was easy travelling, the water being seldom less than two feet deep, and with rocks really visible by the eddy bubbling about them, because they were sharp and jagged. It is the long smooth and round-topped rock which is the most treacherous in a fast river, for the spray which the current throws round such a rock is often not different from an ordinary wave. Now and then the stream was so swift that I was afraid of losing my straw hat, simply from the breeze created by great speed—for it was a day without wind.

It cannot be concealed that continuous physical enjoyment such as this tour presented is a dangerous luxury if it be not properly used. In hours of charming brightness my mind sometimes turned back to workday life and daily duty. When I thought of the hospitals of London, of the herds of squalid poor in fœtid alleys, of the pale-faced ragged boys, and the vice, sadness, pain, and poverty we are sent to do battle with if we be Christian soldiers, I could not help asking, "Am I right in thus enjoying such comfort, such scenery, such health?" Certainly not right, unless to get vigour of thought and hand, and freshened energy of mind, and larger thankfulness and wider love, and so, with all the powers recruited, to enter the field again more eager and able to be useful.[1]

In the more lonely parts of the Reuss the trees were in dense thickets to the water's edge, and the wild ducks fluttered out from them with a splash, and some larger birds like bustards hovered about the canoe. I think among the flying companions there was also the bunting, or "ammer" (from which German word comes our English "yellow hammer") wood pigeon, and very beautiful hawks. The herons and kingfishers were here as well, but not so many of them as on the Danube.

Nothing particular occurred, although it was a pleasant morning's work, until we got through the bridge at Imyl, where an inn was high up on the bank. The ostler helped me to carry the boat into the stable, and the landlady, knowing that her customer would never come again, audaciously charged me 4s. 6d. for my first dinner, for mine was a greedy crew and always had two dinners on full working days.

The navigation after this began to be more interesting, with gravel banks and big stones to avoid, and the channel to be chosen from among several, and the wire ropes of the ferries stretched tightly across the river requiring to be noticed with proper respect. You may have observed how difficult it is sometimes to see a rope when it is stretched tight and horizontal, or at any rate how hard it is to judge correctly of its distance from your eye. This can be well noticed in walking by the seashore among fishing boats moored on the beach, when you will sometimes even knock your nose against a taut hawser before you are aware that it is so close.

This is caused by the fact that the mind estimates the distance of an object partly by comparing the two views of its surface obtained by the two eyes respectively, and which views are not quite the same, but differ, just as the two pictures prepared for the stereoscope. Each eye sees a little round one side of the object, and the solid look of the object and its distance are thus before the mind. Now when the rope is horizontal the eyes do not see round the two sides in this manner, though if the head is leant sideways it will be found that the illusion referred to no longer operates.

Nor is it out of place to inquire thus at length into this matter, for one or two blunt slaps on the head from these ropes across a river make it at least interesting if not pleasant to examine "the reason why." And now we have got the philosophy of the thing, we may let go the ropes.

The actual number of miles in a day's work for the canoeist is much influenced by the number of waterfalls or artificial barriers which are too dry or too high to allow the canoe to float over them.

In all such cases, I had to get out and to drag the boat round by the fields, or to lower her carefully among the rocks, as is shown in the sketch, which represents the usual appearance of that operation. Although this sort of work was a change of posture, and brought into play new muscular action, yet the strain sometimes put on the limbs by the weight of the boat, and the great caution required where there was only slippery footing, made these barriers to be regarded on the whole as bores. Full soon however we were to forget such trifling troubles, for more serious work impended.

The river banks suddenly assumed a new character. They were steep and high, and their height increased as we advanced between the two upright walls of stratified gravel and boulders.

A full body of water ran here, the current being of only ordinary force at its edges, where it was interrupted by rocks, stones, and shingles, and was thus twisted into eddies innumerable. To avoid these entanglements at the sides, it seemed best, on the whole, to keep the boat in mid-channel, though the breakers were far more dangerous there, in the full force of the stream. I began to think that this must be the "hard place" coming, which a wise man farther up the river had warned me was quite too much for so small a boat, unless in flood times, when fewer rocks would be in the way. My reply to this was that when we got near such a place I would pull out my boat and drag it along the bank. "Ah! but the banks are a hundred feet high," he said. So I had mentally resolved (but entirely forgot) to stop in good time and to clamber up the banks and investigate matters ahead before going into an unknown run of broken water.

Such plans are very well in theory, but somehow the approach to these rapids was so gradual, and the mind was so much occupied in overcoming the particular difficulty of each moment that no opportunity occurred for rest or reflection. The dull heavy roar round the corner got louder as the Rob Roy neared the great bend. For here the river makes a turn round the whole of a letter S, in fact very nearly in a complete figure of 8, and in wheeling thus it glides over a sloping ledge of flat rocks, spread obliquely athwart the stream for a hundred feet on either hand, and just a few inches below the surface.

The canoe was swept over this singular place by the current, its keel and sides grinding and bumping on the stones, and sliding on the soft moss, which here made the rock so slippery and black. The progress was aided by sundry pushes and jerks of mine at proper times, but we advanced altogether in a clumsy, helpless style, until at length there came in sight the great white ridge of tossing foam where the din was great, and a sense of excitement and confusion filled the mind.

I was quite conscious that the sight before me was made to look worse because of the noise around, and by the feeling of loneliness and powerlessness of a puny man struggling in a waste of breakers, where to strike on a single one was sure to upset the boat. Here, too, it would evidently be difficult to save the canoe by swimming alongside if she capsized or foundered, and yet it was utterly impossible now to stop.

Right in front, and in the middle, I saw the well-known wave which is always raised when a main stream converges, as it rushes down a narrow neck. The depression or trough of this was about four feet below, and the crest two feet above the level, so the height of the wave was about six feet. Though tall it was thin and sharp featured, and always stationary in position, while the water composing it was going at a tremendous pace. After this wave there was another smaller one, as frequently happens.

It was not the *height* of the wave that gave any concern; had it been at sea the boat would rise over any lofty billow, but here the wave stood still, and the canoe was to be impelled against it with all the force of a mighty stream, and so it must go through the body of water, for it could not have time to rise. And then the question remained, "What is behind that wave?" For if a rock is there then this is the last hour of the Rob Roy.[2]

The boat plunged headlong into the shining mound of

water as I clenched my teeth and clutched my paddle. We saw her sharp prow deeply buried, and then my eyes were shut involuntarily, and before she could rise the mass of solid water struck me with a heavy blow full in the breast, closing round my neck as if cold hands gripped me, and quite taking away my breath.

Vivid thoughts coursed through the brain in this exciting moment, but another slap from the lesser wave, and a whirling round in the eddy below, soon told that the battle was over, and the little Rob Roy slowly rose from under a load of water, which still covered my wrists, and then, trembling, as if stunned by the heavy shock, she staggered to the shore. The river too had done its worse, and it seemed now to draw off from hindering us, and so I clung to a rock to rest for some minutes, panting with a tired thrilling of nervousness and gladness strangely mingled.

Although the weight of the water had been so heavy on my body and legs, very little of it had got inside under the waterproof covering, for the whole affair was done in a few seconds, and though everything in front was completely drenched up to my necktie, the back of my coat was scarcely wet. Most fortunately I had removed the flag from its usual place about an hour before, and thus it was preserved from being swept away.

Well, now it is over, and we are rested, and can begin again with a fresh start; for there is still some work to do in threading among the breakers. The main point, however, has been passed, and the difficulties after it look small, though at other times perhaps they might receive attention. Here is our resting place, the old Roman town of Bremgarten, which is built in a hollow of this very remarkable serpent bend of the rapid Reuss. The houses are stuck on the rocks, and abut the river itself, and as the stream bore me past these I clung to the doorstep of a washerwoman's house, and pulled by boat out of the water into her very kitchen, to the great amusement and surprise of the worthy lady, who wondered still more when I hauled the canoe again through the other side of her room until it fairly came out to the street behind!

It must have astonished the people to see a canoe thus suddenly appearing on their quiet pavement. They soon crowded round and bore her to the hotel, which was a moderately bad one. Next morning the bill was twelve francs, nearly double its proper amount; and thus we encountered in one day the only two extortionate innkeepers met with at all, and even at this second one I made the landlord take eight francs as a compromise.

This quaint old Bremgarten, with high walls and a foss, and antiquities was well worth the inspection of my early morning walk next day, and then the Rob Roy was ordered to the door.

NOTES

1 The crew of the canoe gave eighty-five lectures upon the "Rob Roy on the Jordan," and forty-three lectures on "Underground Adventures," &c., in the whole profits of which, amounting to £10,200 (in January, 1879), were paid to schools, hospitals, churches, asylums, and other institutions in England.

2 I had not then acquired the knowledge of a valuable fact, that a sharp wave of this kind never has a rock behind it. A sharp wave requires free water at its rear, and it is therefore in the safest part of the river so far as concealed dangers are concerned. This at least was the conclusion come to after frequent observations afterwards of many such places.

A faithful representation of the incident on the Reuss, so far as concerns the water, is given in the Frontispiece. In higher flood the river would be faster but smoother, in lower times it would be slower and broken into pools.

CHAPTER IX

Hunger—Music at the Mill—Damsels—Sentiment and Chops—Buying Clothes—The Snags—Shooting a Fall—Fixed—An ex-Courier—Log Bearings—The Drowned Lord—"Wasserfall"—Cow and Canoe—"Valtare Scote"—"Man Preserver."

The wetting and excitement of yesterday made me rather stiff in beginning again; and whenever a rushing sound was heard in front I was aware of a new anxiety as to whether this might not mean the same sort of rough work as yesterday's over again, whereas hitherto this sound of breakers to come had always promised nothing but pleasure. But things very soon came back to their old way, a continuous enjoyment from morning to night.

The river was rapid again, but with no really difficult places. I saw one raft in course of preparation, though there were not many boats, for as the men there said, "How could we get boats up that stream?" The villages near the river were often so high up on lofty cliffs, or otherwise unsuitable, that I went on for some miles trying in vain to find a stopping place. Each bend of the winding water held out hopes that down there at last, or round that bluff cape at farthest, there must be a proper place to breakfast. But when it was now long past the usual hour, and the shores were less inhabited and hunger was more imperative, we determined to land at a mill which overhung the stream in a picturesque spot.

I landed unobserved. This was a blunder in diplomacy, for the canoe is always good as credentials; but I climbed up the bank and through the garden, and found the hall door open; so I walked timidly into a large, comfortable house, leaving my paddle outside lest it might be regarded as a bludgeon. I had come as a beggar, not a burglar.

The chords of a piano, well struck and by firm fingers, led me towards the drawing room; for to hear music is almost to make sure of welcome in a house, and it was so now. My bows and reverences scarcely softened the exceedingly strange appearance I must have made as an intruder, clothed in universal flannel, and offering ten thousand apologies in French, German, and English for thus dropping down from the clouds, that is to say, climbing up from the water.

The young miller rose from the piano, and bowed. His fair sister stopped her sweet song, and blushed. For my part, being only a sort of "casual," I modestly asked for bread and wine, and got hopelessly involved in an effort to explain how I had come by the river unperceived. The excessive courtesy of my new friends was embarrassing, and was further complicated by the arrival of another young lady, even more surprised and hospitable.

Quickly the refreshments were set on the table, and the miller sealed the intimacy by lighting his ample pipe. Our conversation was of the most lively and unintelligible character, and soon lapsed into music, when Beethoven and Goss told all we had to say in chants and symphonies. The inevitable sketch book whiled away a good hour, till the ladies were joined by a third damsel, and the Adventures of Ulysses had to be told to three Penelopes at once. The miller's party became humorous to a degree, and they resisted all my efforts to get away, even when the family dinner was set on the board, and the domestic servants and farm labourers came in to seat themselves at a lower table. This was a picture of rural life not soon to be forgotten.

The stately grandmamma of the mansion now advanced, prim and stiff, and with dignity and matronly grace entreated the stranger to join their company. The old oak furniture was lightened by a hundred little trifles worked by the women, or collected by the tasteful diligence of their brother; and the sun shone, and the mill went round, and the river rolled by, and all was kindness, "because you are an Englishman."

The power of the *Civis Romanus* is far better shown when it draws forth kindness, than when it compels fear. But as respects the formal invitation given above it would not do to stop and eat, and it would not do to stop and not eat, or to make the potatoes get cold, or the granddames' dinner too late; so I *must* go, even though the girls had playfully hidden my luggage to keep the guest among them.

The whole party, therefore, adjourned to the little nook where my boat had been left concealed; and when they caught sight of its tiny form, and its little fluttering flag, the young ladies screamed with delight and surprise, clapping their hands and waving adieux as we paddled away.

I left this happy pleasant scene with mingled feelings, and tried to think out what was the daily life in this sequestered mill; and if my paddling did for a time become a little sentimental, it may be pardoned by travellers who have come among kind friends where they expected perhaps a cold rebuff.

The romantic effect of all this was to make me desperately hungry, for be it known that bread and wine and Beethoven will not do to dine upon if you are rowing forty miles in the sun. So it must be confessed that when, an hour afterwards, I saw an auberge by the water's edge, it became necessary to stifle my feelings by ordering an omelette and two chops. The table was soon spread under a shady pear tree just by the water, and the Rob Roy rested gently on the ripples at my feet. The pleasures of this sunny hour of well-earned repose, freshened by a bunch of grapes and a pear plucked from above my head, were just a little troubled by a slight misapprehension that some day the miller's sister might come by and hear the truth as to how I had sought comfort for my lacerated heart.

Again "to boat," and down by the shady trees, under the towering rocks, over the nimble rapids, and winding among orchards, vineyards, and wholesome scented hay, the same old story of constant varied pleasure. The hills were in front now, and their contour showed that some rivers were to join company with the Reuss, which here rolled on a fine broad stream, like the Thames at Putney. Presently the Limmat flowed in at one side, and at the other the river Aar, which last then gives the name to all the three, though it did not appear to be the largest.

This is not the only Aar among the rivers, but it is the "old original Aar," which Swiss travellers regard as an acquaintance after they have seen it dash headlong over the rocks at Handek. It takes its rise from two glaciers, one of them the Finster Aar glacier, not far from Grimsel; and to me this gave it a special interest, for I had been hard pushed once in the wilds near that homely Hospice.

It was on an afternoon some years ago, when I came from the Furca, by the Rhone glacier to the foot of the valley, walking with two Germans; and as they were rather muffs, and meant to stop there, I thoughtlessly set off alone to climb the rocks and to get to the Grimsel by myself. This is easy enough in daylight, but it was nearly six o'clock when I started, and in October; so after a short half-hour of mounting, the snow began to fall, and the darkness was not made less by the white flakes drifting across it. By some happy conjuncture I managed to scale the pathless mountain, and struck on a little stream which had often to be forded in the dark, but was always leading to the desired valley. At length the light of the Hospice shone welcome as a haven to steer for, and I soon joined the pleasant English guests inside, and bought a pair of trousers from the waiter at 3s. 6d. for a change in the wet.

But paddling on the Aar had no great danger where we met it now, for the noisy, brawling torrent was sobered by age, and after much knocking about in the world it had settled into a steady and respectable river. A few of my friends, the snags, were, however, lodged in the water hereabouts, and as they bobbed their heads in uneasy beds, and the river was much discoloured, it became quite worth while to keep a sharp lookout for these dangerous companions.

The "river tongue," explained already as consisting of sign language with a parallel comment in loud English, was put to a severe test on a wide stream like this. Consider, for example, how you could best ask the following question (speaking by signs and English only) from a man who is on the bank over there a hundred yards away.

"Is it better for me to go over to those rocks, and keep on the left of that island, or to pull my boat out at these stumps, and drag her on land into this channel?"

One comfort is the man made out my meaning, for he did not answer, "Jo wohl?" He would not have done more had we both learned the same language, even if he had heard what I said.

Mills occurred here and there. Some of these had the waterwheel simply built on the river; others had it so arranged as to allow the shaft to be raised or lowered to suit the varying height of water in floods and droughts. Others had it floating on barges. Others, again, had a half weir built diagonally across part of the river; and it was important to look carefully at this wall so as to see on which side it ought to be kept in selecting the best course. In a few cases there was another construction; two half weirs, converged gradually towards the middle of the river, forming a letter V, with its sharp end turned *up* the stream, and leaving a narrow opening, there, through which a torrent flowed, with rough waves dancing merrily in the pool below. I had to "shoot" several of these, and at other times, in the manner explained before.

On one occasion I was in an unaccountably careless fit, and instead of first examining the depth of the water on the edge of the little fall, I resolved to go straight at it and take my chance.

It must be stated that while a depth of three inches is enough for the canoe to float in when all its length is in the water, the same depth will by no means suffice at the upper edge of a fall. For when the boat arrives there the fore part, say six or seven feet of it, projects for a time over the fall and out of the water, and is merely in the air, without support, so that the centre of the keel will sink at least six or seven inches; and if there be not more water than this the keel catches the crest of the weir, and the boat will then stop, and perhaps swing round, after which it must fall over sideways, unless considerable dexterity is used in the management.

Although a case of this sort had occurred to me before, I got again into the same predicament, which was made far more puzzling as the fore end of the boat went under a rock at the bottom of the fall, and thus the canoe hung upon the edge, and would go neither one way nor another.[1] It would also have been very difficult to get out of the boat in this position; for to jump feet foremost would have broken the boat—to plunge in head first on the rocks below would have broken my head.

The canoe was much wrenched in my struggles, which ended, however, by man and boat tumbling down sideways, and, marvelous to say, quite safely to the lower level. This performance was not one to be proud of. Surely it was like ingratitude to treat the Rob Roy thus, exposing it to needless risk when it had carried me so far and so well.

The Aar soon flows into the Rhine, and here is our canoe on old Rhenus once more, with the town of Waldshut ("end of the forest") leaning over the high bank to welcome us near. There is a lower path and a row of little houses at the bottom of the cliff, past which the Rhine courses with rapid eddies deep and strong. Here an old fisherman soon espied me, and roared out his biography at the top of his voice; how he had been a courier in Lord Somebody's family; how he had journeyed seven years in Italy, and could fish with artificial flies, and was seventy years old, with various other reasons why I should put my boat into his house.

He was just the man for the moment; but first those two uninformed *douaniers* must be dealt with, and I had to satisfy their dignity by paddling up the strong current to their lair; for the fly had touched the spider's web and the spiders were too grand to come out and seize it. Good humour, and smiles, and a little judicious irony as to the absurd notion of overhauling a canoe which could be carried on your back, soon made them release me, if only to uphold their own dignity, and I left the boat in the best drawing room of the ex-courier, and ascended the hill to the hotel aloft. But the man came too, and he had found time to prepare an amended report of the boat's journey for the worthy landlord, so, as usual, there was soon everything ready for comfort and good cheer.

Waldshut is made up of one wide street almost closed at the end, and with pretty gardens about it, and a fine prospect from its high position; but an hour's walk appeared to exhaust all the town could show, though the scenery round such a place is not to be done with in this brief manner.

The visitors soon came to hear and see more nearly what the newspapers had told them of the canoe. One gentleman, indeed, seemed to expect me to unfold the boat from my pocket, for a French paper had spoken about a man going over the country "with a canoe under his arm." The evening was enlivened by some signals, which burned at my bedroom window to lighten up the street, which little entertainment was evidently quite new to the Waldshutians.

Before we start homewards on the Rhine with our faces due West, it may be well very briefly to give the log bearings and direction of the canoe's voyage up to this point.

First, by the Thames, July 29, E. (East), to Shoeburyness, thence to Sheerness, S. From thence by rail to Dover, and by steamer to Ostend, and rail again, Aug. 7, to the Meuse, along which the course was nearly E., until its turn into Holland, N.E. Then, Aug. 11, to the Rhine, S.E., and ascending it nearly S., until at Frankfort, Aug. 17, we go N.E. by rail to Asschaffenburg, and by the river wind back again to Frankfort in wide curves. Farther up the Rhine, Aug. 25, our course is due S., till from Freyburg the boat is carted E. to the Titisee, and to Donaueschingen, and Aug. 28, descends the Danube, which there flows nearly E., but with great bends to N. and S., until, Sept. 2, we are at Ulm. The rail next carries us S. to the Lake of Constance, which is sailed along in a course S.W., and through the Zeller See to Schaffhausen, Sept. 7, it was about W. Thence turning S. to Zurich, and over the lake and the neck of land, and veering to the W. by Zug, we arrive on the Lucerne, Sept. 10, where the southernmost point of the voyage is reached, and then our prow points to N., till, on Sept. 12, we land at Waldshut.

This devious course had taken the boat to several different kingdoms and states—Holland, Belgium, France, Wurtemburg, Bavaria, and the Grand Duchy of Baden, Rhenish, Prussia, the Palatinate, Switzerland, and the pretty Hohenzollern Sigmaringen. Now we had come back again to the very Grand Duchy again, a land wherein all travellers must mind their p's and q's.

The ex-courier took the canoe from his wife's washing tubs and put her on the Rhine, and then he spirited my start by recounting the lively things we must expect soon afterwards to meet. I must take care to "keep to the right," near the falls of Lauffenburg, for an English lord had been carried over them and drowned;[2] and I must be aware of Rheinfelden rapids, because an Englishman had tried to descend them in a boat with a fisherman, and their craft was capsized and the fisherman was drowned; and I must do this here, and that there, and so many other things everywhere else, that all the directions were jumbled up together. But it seemed to relieve the man to tell his tale, and doubtless he sat down to his breakfast comfortable in mind and body, and cut his meat into little bits, and then changed the fork to the right hand to eat them every one, as they all do hereabouts, with every appearance of content.

Up with the sails! for the East wind freshens, and the fair wide river hurries us along. This was a splendid scene to sail in, with lofty banks of rock, and rich meads, or terraces laden with grapes. After a good morning's pleasure here the wind suddenly rose to a gale, and I took in my jib just in time, for a sort of minor hurricane came on, raising tall columns of dust on the road alongside, blowing off men's hats, and whisking up the hay and leaves and branches high into the air.

Still we kept our lug sail set; and with wind and current in the same direction I scudded faster than I ever sailed before in my life. Great exertion was required to manage a light skiff safely with such a whirlwind above and a whirlwater below; one's nerves were kept in extreme tension, and it was a hurried half-hour of pleasant excitement.

For this reason it was that I did not for some time notice a youth who had been running after the boat, yelling and shrieking, and waving his coat in the air. We drew nearer to him, and then luffed up, hailing him with, "What's the matter?" and he could only pant out, "Wasserfall, Wasserfall, fünf minuten!"—the breeze had brought me within a hundred yards of the falls of Lauffenburg—the whistle of the wind had drowned the roar of the water.

I crossed to the right bank (as the ex-courier had directed), but the youth's loud cries to come to the "links," or left side, at last prevailed, and he was right in this. The sail was soon lowered, and the boat was hauled on a raft, and then this fine young fellow explained that two minutes more would have turned the corner and drawn me into the horrid current sweeping over the falls.

While he set off in search of a cart to convey the boat, I had time to pull her up the high bank and make all snug for a drive, and soon he returned with a very grotesque carter and a most crazy vehicle, actually drawn by a milch cow! All three of us laughed as we hoisted the Rob Roy on this cart, and the cow kicked vehemently, either at the cart, or the boat, or the laughing.

Our procession soon entered the little town, but it was difficult to be dignified. As the cart with a screeching wheel rattled slowly over the big round stones of the street, vacant at mid-day, the windows were soon full of heads, and after one peep at us, down they rushed to see the fun. A cow drawing a boat to the door of a great hotel is certainly a quaint proceeding; although in justice to the worthy quadruped I should mention that she now behaved in a proper and ladylike manner.

Here the public hit upon every possible way but the right one to pronounce the boat's name, which was painted in blue letters on her bow. Some people read it "Road Ro," and others "Rubree," but at length a man in spectacles called out, "Ah! ah! Valtarescote!" The mild Sir Walter's novels had not been written in vain.

The falls of Lauffenburg[3] can be seen well from the bridge which spans the river, much narrowed at this spot. A raft is coming down as we look at the thundering foam—of course without the men upon it; see the great solid frame that seems to resent the quickening of its quiet pace, and to hold back with a presentiment of evil as every moment draws it nearer to the plunge.

Crash go all the bindings, and the huge, sturdy logs are hurled topsy-turvy into the gorge bouncing about like chips of firewood and rattling among the foam. Nor was it easy to look calmly on this without thinking how the frail canoe would have fared in such a cauldron of cold water boiling. The salmon drawn into this place get terribly puzzled by it, and so they are caught by hundreds in great iron cages lowered from the rocks for this purpose. Fishing stations of the same kind are found at several points on the river, where a stage is built on piles, and a beam supports a strong net below. In a little house, like a sentry box, you notice a man seated, silent and lonely, while he holds tenderly in his hand a dozen strings, which are fastened to the edges of the net. When a fish is beguiled into the snare, or is borne in by swift current bewildering, the slightest vibrations of the net are thrilled along the cords to the watcher's hand, and then he raises the great beam and secures the prize.

My young friend, who had kindly warned me, and hired the cow, and shown the salmon, I now invited to breakfast, and he became the hero of the hour, being repeatedly addressed by the other inquirers in an unpronounceable German title, which signifies, in short, "Man preserver." Here we heard again of a certain four-oared boat with five Englishmen in it, which had been sent out from London overland to Schaffhausen, and then rowing swiftly down the Rhine, had come to Lauffenburg about six weeks before, and I fully sympathized with the crew in their charming pull, especially if the weather was such as we had enjoyed; that is to say, not one shower in the boat from the source of the Danube to the Palace of Westminster.

NOTES

1 This adventure was the result of temporary carelessness, while that at the rapids was the result of impatience, for the passage of these latter could probably have been effected without encountering the central wave had proper time been spent in examining the place. Let not any tourist then be deterred from a paddle on the Reuss, which is a perfectly suitable river, with no avoidable dangers.

2 This was Lord Montague, the last of his line, and on the same day his family mansion of Cowdray, in Sussex, was burned to the ground.

3 "Lauffenburg" means the "town of the falls," from "laufen," to turn; and the Yankee term "loafer" may come from this, "herum laufer," one running about.

CHAPTER X

A Field of Foam—Precipice—Puzzled—Philosophy—
Rheinfelden Rapids—Dazzled—Jabbering—Blissful Ignorance
—Astride—Find a Way—Very Salt—
Bright Lad—German Friend—The Whirlpool
—Cauliflower—Bride and Baby—"Squar."

The canoe was now fixed on a handcart and dragged once more through the streets to a point below the falls, and the Rob Roy became very lively on the water after her few hours of rest. All was brilliant around, and deep underneath, and azure above, and happy within, till the dull distant sound of breakers began again and soon got louder, and at last was near, and could not be ignored; we have come to the rapids of Rheinfelden.

The exaggeration with which judicious friends at each place describe the dangers to be encountered is so general in these latitudes that one learns to receive it calmly, but the scene itself when I came to the place was certainly puzzling and grand.

Imagine a thousand acres of water in white crested waves, varied only by black rocks resisting a struggling torrent, and a loud, thundering roar, mingled with a strange hissing, as the spray from ten thousand sharp-pointed billows is tossed into the air.

And then you are alone too, and the banks are high, and you have a precious boat to guard.

While there was time to do it I stood up in my boat to survey, but it was a mere horizon of waves, and nothing could be learned from looking. Then I coasted towards one side where the shrubs and trees hanging in the water brushed the paddle, and seemed to be so safe because they were on shore.

The rapids of Bremgarten could probably be passed most easily by keeping to the edge, though with much delay and numerous "getting outs," but an attempt now to go along the side in this way was soon shown to be useless, for presently I came to a lofty rock jutting out into the stream, and the very loud roar behind it fortunately attracted so much attention that I pulled into the bank, made the boat fast, and mounted through the thickset to the top of the cliff.

I saw at once that to try to pass by this rock in any boat would be madness, for the swiftest part of the current ran right under the projecting crag, and then wheeled round and plunged over a height of some feet into a pool of foam, broken fragments, and powerful waves.

But, stay, would it be just possible to float the boat past the rock while I might hold the painter from above? The rock on careful measurement was found too high for this.

To see well over the cliff I had to lie down on my face, and the pleasant curiosity felt at first, as to how I should have to act, now gradually sickened into the sad conviction, "Impossible!" Then was the time to turn with earnest eyes to the wide expanse of river, and to see if haply, somewhere at least, even in the middle, a channel might be traced. Yes, there certainly was a channel, only one, very far out, and very difficult to hit upon when you sit in a boat quite near the level of the water; but the attempt must now be made, or—might I not get the boat carried round by land? Under the trees far off were men who might be called to help, labourers quietly working and never minding me. I was tempted, but did not yield.

For a philosophical thought had come upmost, that, after all, the boat had not to meet *every* wave and rock now visible, and the thousand breakers dashing around, but only a certain few, which would be on each side in my crooked and untried way; in fact that of the rocks in any one line—say fifty of them between me and any point—only two would become a new danger in crossing that line.

Then, again, rapids look worse from the shore than they really are, because you see all their difficulties at once, and you hear the general din. On the other hand, waves look much smaller from the bank (being hidden by others) than you find them to be when the boat is in the trough between two. Thus, the hidden rocks may make a channel, that looks good enough from the land, to be quite impracticable when you attempt it in the water.

Lastly, the current is seen to be swifter from the shore where you can observe its speed from a fixed point, than it seems when you are in the water where you notice only its velocity in relation to the stream on each side, which is itself all the time running at four or five miles an hour. But it is the positive speed of the current that ought really to be considered, for it is by this the boat will be urged against a breaker stationary in the river.

To get to this middle channel at once from the place where I had left my boat was not possible. We must enter it higher up the river, so I had to pull the canoe up stream, over shallows, and along the bristly margin, wading, towing, and struggling, for about half a mile, till at length it seemed we must be high enough up stream to let me paddle out swiftly across, while the current would take the boat sideways to the rough water.

And now in a little quiet bay I rested half an hour to recover strength after this exertion, and to prepare fully for a "spurt," which might indeed be delayed in starting, but which, once begun, must be vigorous and watchful to the end.

Here various thoughts blended and tumbled about in the mind most disorderly. To leave this quiet bank and willingly rush out, in cold blood, into a field of white breakers; to tarnish the fair journey with a foolhardy prank; to risk the Rob Roy where the touch of one rock was utter destruction. Will it be pleasant? Can it be wise? Is it right?

The answer was, to sponge out every drop of water from the boat, to fasten the luggage inside, that it might not fall out in an upset, to brace the waterproof cover all tight around, and to get its edge in my teeth ready to let go in capsizing—and then to pull one gentle stroke which put the boat's nose out of the quiet water into the fast stream, and hurrah! we are off at a swinging pace.

The sun, now shining exactly up stream, was an exceedingly uncomfortable addition to the difficulties; for its glancing beams confounded all the horizon in one general band of light, so that rocks, waves, solid water, and the most flimsy foam were all the same at a little distance. This, the sole disadvantage of a cloudless sky, was so much felt in my homeward route that I sometimes prolonged the morning's work by three or four hours (with the sun behind or on one side), so as to shorten the evening's *quota* where it was dead in the eye of the sun. On the present occasion, when it was of great moment to hit the channel exactly, I could not see it at all, even with my blue spectacles on. They seemed to be utterly powerless against such a fiery blaze; and, what was almost worse, my eyes were thereby so dazzled that on looking to nearer objects I could scarcely see them either.

This unexpected difficulty was so serious that I thought for a moment of keeping on in my present course (directed across the river), so as to attain the opposite side, and there to wait for the sun to go down. But it was already too late to adopt this plan, for the current had been swiftly bearing me down stream, and an instant decision must be made. "Now," thought I, "judging by the number of paddle strokes, we must surely be opposite the channel in the middle, and now I must turn to it."

By a happy hit, the speed and the direction of the canoe were both well fitted, so that when the current had borne us to the breakers the boat's bow was just turned exactly down stream, and I entered the channel whistling, for very loneliness, like a boy in the dark.

But it was soon seen to be "all right, Englishmen;" so in ten minutes more the canoe had passed the rapids, and we floated along pleasantly on that confused bobbery of little billows always found below broken water—a very mob of waves, which for a time seem to be elbowing and jostling in all directions to find their proper places.

I saw here two fishermen by one of the salmon traps described above, and at once pulled over to them, to land on a little white bank of sand, that I might rest, and bale out, and hear the news. The men asked if I had come down the rapids in that boat. "Yes." "By the middle channel?" "Yes." They smiled to each other and then both at once commenced a most voluble and loudspoken address in the vilest of patois. Their eagerness and energy rose to such a pitch that I began to suppose they were angry; but the upshot of all this eloquence (always louder when you are seen not to understand one word of it) was this, "There are rapids to come.

You will get there in half an hour. They are far worse than what you have passed. Your boat *must* be carried round them on land."

To see if this was said to induce me to employ them as porters, I asked the men to come along in their boat, so as to be ready to help me; but they consulted together, and did not by any means agree in admiring this proposal. Then I asked them to explain the best route through the next rapids, when they drew such confused diagrams on the sand, and gave such complicated directions, that it was impossible to make head or tail of their atrocious jargon; so I quietly bowed, wiped out the sand pictures with my foot, and started again happy and free; for it is really the case that in these things "ignorance is bliss." The excitement of finding your way, and the satisfaction when you have found it yourself, is well worth all the trouble. Just so in mountain travel. If you go merely to work the muscles, and to see the view, it will do to be tied by a rope to three guides, and to follow behind them; but then theirs is all the mental exertion, and tact, and judgment, while yours is only the merit of keeping up with the leaders, treading in their steps. And therefore I have observed that there is less of this particular pleasure of the discoverer when one is ascending Mont Blanc, where by traditional rule you must be tied to the guides, than in making out a path over a mountain pass undirected and alone, though the heights thus climbed are not so great.

When the boat got near the lower rapids, I went ashore and walked for half a mile down the bank, and so was able to examine the bearings well. It appeared practicable to get along by the shallower parts of one side, so this was resolved upon as my course. It is surely quite fair to go by the easiest way, provided there is no carrying overland adopted, or other plan for shirking the water. The method accordingly used in this case was rather a novel mode of locomotion, and it was quite successful, as well as highly amusing.

In the wide plain of breakers here, the central district seemed radically bad, so we cautiously kept out of the main current, and went where the stream ran fast enough nevertheless. I sat stridelegs on the deck of the boat near its stern, and was thus floated down until the bow, projecting out of the water, went above a ridge of rocks, and the boat grounded. Thus the shock was received against my legs hanging in the water, so that the violence of its blow was eased from the boat. Standing, then, with both feet on the rock, while the canoe went free from between my knees she could be lowered down or pushed forward until the water got deeper, and when it got too deep to wade after her the Rob Roy was pulled back between my knees, and I sat down again on the deck as before.

The chief difficulty in this proceeding was to be equally attentive at once to keep hold of the boat, to guide it between rocks, to keep hold of the paddle, and to manage not to tumble on loose stones, or to get into the water above the waist.

Thus by successive riding and ferrying over the deep pools, and walking and wading in the shallows, by pushing the boat here, and by being carried upon it there, the lower rapids of Rheinfelden were most successfully passed without any damage.

It will be seen from the description already given of the rapids at Bremgarten, and now of these two rapids on the Rhine, that the main difficulties are only for him who goes there uninformed, and that these can be avoided by examining them on the spot at the cost of a walk and a short delay. But the pleasure is so much enhanced by the whole thing being novel, that, except for a man who wishes simply to *get past*, it is much better to seek a channel for yourself, even if a much easier one has been found out by other people.[1]

The town of Rheinfelden was now in view, and we began to wonder how the English four-oar boat we had traced as far as Lauffenburg could have managed to descend the rapids just now passed. But we learned afterwards that the four-oar had come there in a time of flood, when rocks would be covered, and probably with only such eddies as we had already noticed higher up the river where it was deep. So they pulled on bravely to Bale, where the hotel folks mentioned that when the five moist Britons arrived their clothes and baggage were all drenched, and the waiter said, with a malicious grin, that thereby his friend the washerwoman had earned twenty-seven francs in one night. I steered to a large building with a smooth gravel shore in front—the salt water baths of Rheinfelden—a favourite resort for crippled invalids. The salt rock in the earth beneath impregnates the springs with such an intensity of brine that eight percent of fresh water has to be added before the saline mixture can be medicinally employed as a bath. If you take a glass of the water as it comes from the spring, and put a little salt in it, the salt will not dissolve, for the water is already saturated, and a drop of it put on your coat speedily dries up and leaves a white stain of minute crystals. In fact, this water seemed to me to be far more saline than even the water of the Dead Sea, which is in all conscience salt enough, as every one knows who has rubbed it on his face in that reeking hot death-stricken valley of Jericho.

Though the shore was pleasant here and the water was calm, there was no one to welcome me now, and yet this was the only time I had reason to expect somebody to greet the arrival of the canoe. For in the morning a worthy German had told me he was going by train to Rheinfelden, and he would keep a look out for the canoe, and would surely meet me there if we "ever got through the rapids." But he said afterwards that he *had* come there, and with his friends, too, and they had waited and waited till at last they gave up the Rob Roy as a "missing ship." Excellent man, he must have had some novel excuses to comfort his friends as they retired, disappointed, after waiting in vain!

There was, however, not far off, a poor woman washing clothes by the river, and thumping and bullying them with a wooden bludgeon as if her sole object was to smash up the bachelor's shirt buttons. A fine boy of eight years old was with her, a most intelligent little fellow, whose quick eye at once caught sight of the Rob Roy as it dashed round the point and landed me there a tired, tanned traveller, wet and warm.

This juvenile helped me more than any man ever did, and with such alacrity, too, and intelligence, and good humour, that I felt grateful to the boy. We spread out the sails to dry, and my socks and shoes in the sun, and sponged out the boat, and then dragged her up the high bank. Here, by good luck, we found two wheels on an axle left alone, for what purpose I cannot imagine; but we got a stick and fastened it to them as a pole, and put the boat on this extemporized vehicle—the boy having duly got permission from his mamma—and then we pulled the canoe to the gates of the old town, rattling through the streets, even to the door of the hotel. A bright franc in the lad's hand made him start with amaze, but he instantly rose to the dignity of the occasion, and some dozens of other urchins formed an attentive audience as he narrated over and over the events of the last half-hour, and ended always by showing the treasure in his hand, "and the Herr gave me this!"

The Krone hotel here is very prettily situated. It is a large house, with balconies overlooking the water, and a babbling *jet d'eau* in its garden, which is close by the river. The stream flows fast in front, and retains evidence of having passed through troublous times higher up; therefore it makes no small noise as it rushes under the arches of the covered wooden bridge, but though there are rocks and a few eddies the passage is easy enough, if you look at it for five minutes, to form a mental chart of your course. My German friend having found out that the canoe had arrived after all, his excitement and pleasure abounded. Now he was proved right. Now his promises, broken as it seemed all day, were all fulfilled.

He was a very short, very fat, and very hilarious personage, with a minute smattering of English, which he had to speak loudly, so as to magnify its value among his Allemand friends, envious of his accomplishment. His explanations of the contents of my sketch book were truly ludicrous as he dilated on it page by page, but he well deserved all gratitude for ordering my hotel bedroom and its comforts, which were never more acceptable than now after a hard day's work. Music finished the evening, and then the hum of the distant rapids sung me a lullaby breathing soft slumber.

Next morning, as there was but a short row to Bâle, I took a good long rest in the bed, and then carried the canoe half way across the bridge where a picturesque island is formed into a terraced garden, and here we launched the boat on the water. Although the knocks and strains of the last few days were very numerous, and many of them of portentous force, judging by the sounds they made, the Rob Roy was still hale and hearty, and the carpenter's mate had no damages to report to the captain. It was not until harder times came, in the remainder of the voyage, that her timber suffered and her planks were tortured by rough usage.

A number of ladies patronized the start on this occasion, and as they waved their parasols and the men shouted Hoch! and Bravo! We glided downstream, the yellow paddle being waved round my head in an original mode of "salute," which was invented specially for returning friendly gratulations.

Speaking about Rheinfelden, Baedeker says, "Below the town another rapid of the Rhine forms a sort of whirlpool called the Hollenhaken," a formidable announcement and a terrible name; but what is called here a "whirlpool" is not worth notice.

The sound of a railway train beside the river reminds you that this is not quite a strange, wild, unseen country. Reminds you, I say, because really when you are in the river bed you easily forget all that is beyond each side. Let a landscape be ever so well known from the road, it becomes new again when you view it from the level of the water. For any scene, looked at from land, is bounded by a semicircle with the diameter on the horizon, and the arch of sky for its circumference. But when you are seated in the canoe, the picture changes to the form of a great sector, with its point on the clear water, and each radius inclining aloft through the rocks, trees, and mossy banks, on this side and on that. And this holds good even on a well-worn river like the Thames. The land scenes between Oxford and London get pretty well known and admired by travellers, but the views of the same places will seem both fresh and fair if you row down the river through them. There are few streams which have such lovely scenery as the Thames can show in its windings.

But our canoe is now getting back to civilization, and away from that pleasant simplicity where everything done in the streets or the hotel is strange to a stranger. Here as a contrast we have composite candles, and therefore no snuffers; here the waiter insists on speaking English, and so, sitting down by me, and clutching my arm, he confidently announces that there are no "bean green" (translating "haricots verts", but that perhaps I might like a "flower caul," so we assent to a cauliflower.

It is amusing again when the woman waiter of some inland German village shouts louder German to you, because the words she rattles out at first have not been understood. She gazes with a new sensation at a guest who actually cannot comprehend her voluble clatter, and then both guest and waiter have a chorus of laughter.

But now also I saw a boat towed along the Rhine—a painful evidence of being near commerce, even though it was in a primitive style; not that there was any towing path, for the men walked among the bushes, pulling the boat with a rope, and often wading to do so. This sight of another boat, however, told me at once that I had left the fine free forests where you might land anywhere, and it was sure to be lonely and charming.

After a few bends westward we come in sight of the two towers of Bâle, but the setting sun makes it almost impossible to see anything in its brightness, so we must paddle on.

The bridge at Bâle was speedily covered by the idle and the curious as the canoe pulled up at an hotel by the water on Sept. 14. It was here that the four-oared boat had arrived some weeks before with its moist crew. The proprietor of the house was therefore much pleased to see another English boat come in, so little and so lonely, so comfortable and so dry. I walked about the town and entered a church (Protestant here of course), where a number of people had assembled at a baptism. The baby was fixed on a sort of frame, so as to be easily handed about from mother to father, and from clerk to minister; I hereby protest against this mechanical arrangement as a flagrant indignity to the little darling, having myself a great respect for babies, sometimes, a certain awe.

The instant the christening was done, a happy couple came forward to be married, an exceedingly clumsy dolt of a bridegroom and a fair bride, not very young, that is to say, about fifty-five years old. There were no bridesmaids or other perplexing appurtenances, and after the ceremony the couple just walked away, amid the titters of a crowd of women. The bridegroom did not seem to know exactly what to do next. He walked before his wife, then behind her, and then on one side, but it did not somehow feel quite comfortable, so he assumed a sort of diagonal position, and kept nudging her on till they disappeared in some house. Altogether, I never saw a more unromantic commencement of married life, yet there was this redeeming point, that they were not bored by that dread affliction—a marriage breakfast—the first meeting of two jealous sets of new relations, who are all expected to be made friends at once by eating when they are not hungry, and listening when there is nothing to say. But it is not proper for me to criticize these mysteries, so let us go back to the inn. In the coffee room we find a Frenchman, who has been in London, and is now instructing two Mexicans, who are going there, as to hotels. Tis droll to hear his descriptions of the London "Caffy Hous," and the hotels in "Lycestersquar." He said, "It is pronounced *squar* in England."

NOTES
1 Several canoeists have since passed the Rheinfelden rapids, but an upset has been the rule. A Rob Roy canoe has successfully passed the Lachine rapids in Canada, and two others have gone down a swift river lately in Japan. Among all the 600 members of the Royal Canoe Club only one, so far as is known, has been drowned in a canoe voyage.

CHAPTER XI

Which way?—Music in Jungle—Byron—Drawbridges—Gros Kembs Thunderer—Thoroughly dull—Fifty Locks—The Bother at them—Thoughts—An odd Fish—Night Notes—Madame Nico—Tedious—Stared at—The Lady Cow—New Wine

Bâle is, in every sense, a turning point on the Rhine. The course of the river here bends abruptly from west to north, and the character of the scenery beside it alters at once from high sloping banks to a widespread network of streams, all entangled in countless islands, and yet ever tending forward, northward, seaward through the great rich valley of the Rhine with mountain chains along each side, two everlasting barriers. Here then we could start anew almost in any direction, and I had not settled yet what route to take, whether by the Saône and Doubs to paddle to the Rhone, and so descend to Marseilles, and then coast by the Cornici road, and sell the boat at Genoa; or—and some other plan would surely be a better alternative, if it avoids a sale of the Rob Roy—I could not part with her now—so let us decide to go back through France.

We were yet on the river slowly paddling when this decision was arrived at, because I would not leave the pleasant current for a slow canal, until the last possible opportunity. A diligent study of new maps, procured at Bâle, showed that a canal ran northward parallel to the Rhine, and approached very near to the river at one particular spot, which indeed looked hard enough to find even on the map, but was far more dubious when we got into a maze of streamlets and little rivers circling among high osiers, so thick that it was impossible to see a few yards. But the line of tall poplars along the canal was visible now and then, whereby I made a guesswork turn, and thus we got so near the canal that by winding about for a little in a pretty limpid stream, Rob Roy came at last within carrying distance. I knew very well that a song and a whistle on my fingers would be sure to bring anybody out of the osiers who was within reach of the concert, and so it proved, for a woman's head soon peered over a break in the dense cover. She wished to carry the boat, but the skipper's gallantry had scruples as to this proposal, so she fetched a man, and we bore the canoe through hedges and bushes, and over dykes and ditches, and deep grassy fields, till she was safely placed on the canal.

The man was delighted by a two-franc piece; he had been well paid for listening to bad music. As for the boat, she lay still and resigned, awaiting our next move, and as for me, I sighed while giving a last look backward, and said in Byron's lines—

"Adieu to thee, fair Rhine! How long delighted
  The stranger fain would linger on his way!
  Thine is a scene alike where souls united
  Or lonely contemplation thus might stray;

And could the ceaseless vultures cease to prey
On self-condemning bosoms, it were here,
Where Nature, nor too sombre nor too gay,
Wild but not rude, awful yet not austere,
Is to the mellow earth as autumn to the year.

"Adieu to thee again! a vain adieu!
   There can be no farewell to scene like thine;
   The mind is colour'd by thy every hue;
   And if reluctantly the eyes resign
   Their cherish'd gaze upon thee, lovely Rhine!
   'Tis with the thankful glance of parting praise;
   More mighty spots may rise, more glaring shine,
   But none unite in one attaching maze
The brilliant, fair, and soft—the glories of old days.

"The negligently grand, the fruitful bloom
   Of coming ripeness, the white city's sheen,
   The rolling stream, the precipice's gloom,
   The forest's growth, and gothic walls between,
   The wild rocks shaped as they had turrets been
   In mockery of man's art; and these withal
   A race of faces happy as the scene,
   Whose fertile bounties here extend to all,
Still springing o'er thy banks, though empires near them
      fall.

"But these recede. Above me are the Alps,
   The palaces of nature, whose vast walls
   Have pinnacled in clouds their snowy scalps,
   And throned eternity in icy halls
   Of cold sublimity, where forms and falls
   The avalanche—the thunderbolt of snow!

> All that expands the spirit, yet appalls,
> Gather around these summits, as to show
> How earth may pierce to heaven, yet leave vain man below."
> —*Childe Harold*, Canto iii

To my pleasant surprise the canal had a decided current in it, going in the right direction about two miles an hour; and though the little channel was hardly twelve feet wide, yet it was clear and deep, and by no means stupid to travel on. After a few miles we reached a drawbridge, which rested within a foot of the water. A man came to raise the bridge by machinery, and he wondered at my better way of passing it; by shoving my boat under the bridge, while I walked over the top and got into the boat at the other side. Doubtless the Rob Roy was the first boat which had gone under that bridge; but I had passed several very low bridges on the Danube, some of them not two inches above the water, and in these cases the Rob Roy went *over* the bridge. It may be asked, how do such low bridges fare in flood times? Why, the water simply overflows them. In some cases the planks which form the roadway are removed when the water rises, and then the wayfaring man who comes to the river must manage somehow, but his bridge is removed at the very time when the high water makes it necessary.

The bridge man was so intelligent in his remarks that we determined to stop there and breakfast, so I found my way to a little public house at the hamlet of Gros Kembs, and helped the wizened old lady who ruled there to make me an omelette—my help, by the by, consisted in ordering, eating, and paying for the omelette, for the rest she was sure to do well enough, as all French women can.

The village gossips soon arrived, and each person who

saw the boat came on to the inn to see the foreigner who could sail such a *bateau*. The courteous and respectful behavior of Continental people is so uniform that the stranger among them is bound, I think, to amuse and to interest these folk in return. This was most easily done by showing all my articles of luggage, and of course the drawings. A Testament with gilt leaves was, however, the chief object of curiosity, and all the *savants* of the party tried in turn to read it.

One of these as spokesman, and with commendable gravity, told me he had read in their district newspaper about the canoe, but he "little expected to have the honour of meeting its owner." Fancy the local organ of such a place! Is it called the "News of the Wold," or the "Gros Kembs Thunderer"? Well, whatever was the title of the gazette, it had an article about Pontius Pilate and my visit to the Titisee in the Black Forest, and this it was no doubt which had made these canal people so very inquisitive on the occasion.

The route now lay through the great forest of La Hardt, with dense thickets on each side of the canal, and not a sound anywhere to be heard but the hum now and then of a dragon-fly. One or two woodmen met me as they trudged silently home from work, but there was a lonely feeling about the place without any of the romance of wild country. I had to push on, however, and sometimes, for a change, to tow the boat while I walked. In the most brilliant day the scenery of a canal has at best but scant liveliness, the whole thing is so prosaic and artificial, and in fact stupid, if indeed one can ever call a place stupid where there is fresh air and clear water, and blue sky and green trees. Still the difference between a glorious river encircling you with lofty rocks and this canal confining with its earthen walls, was something like that between walking among high mountains and being shut up by mistake in Bloomsbury Square.

No birds chirped or sung, or even flew past, only the buzz-

A Thousand Miles in the Rob Roy Canoe

ing of flies was mingling with the distant shriek of a railway train. It is this iron road that has killed the canal, for I saw no boats moving upon the water. The long continued want of rain had also reduced its powers of accommodation for traffic, and the traffic is so little at best that it would not pay to buy water for the supply. For in times of drought canal water is very expensive. It is said that the Regent's Canal, in London, had to pay 5000£ for what they required one very dry summer.

At length we came to a wide fork of the canal in a basin, and I went along the branch to the town of Mulhouse, a place of great wealth, the largest French cotton town—the Manchester of France, but now bold Germany's. The street boys here were very troublesome, partly because they were intelligent, and therefore inquisitive, and partly because manufacturing towns make little urchins precocious and forward in their manners.

I hired a truck from a woman and hired a man to drag it, and so we took the boat to the large hotel, where they at once recognized the canoe, and seemed to know all about it from report.

Next morning when we took Rob Roy into the railway office as usual and placed her on the counter with the trunks and bandboxes, the officials declined to put her on the train. This was the first time the canoe had been refused on a railroad, and I used every kind of persuasion, but in vain, and this being the first application of the kind on French soil we felt it was a bad precedent, and that difficulties were ahead.

The French railways would not then take a canoe as baggage, while the other seven or eight countries we had brought the boat through were all amenable to pressure on this point, but the French too are wiser now, since other paddlers have journeyed there.

We had desired to go by the railway only a few miles,

but it would have enabled me to avoid about fifty locks on the canal and thus have saved two tedious days. As, however, they would not take the boat in a passenger train we carried her back to the canal, and I determined to face the locks boldly, and to regard them as an exercise of patience and of the flexor muscles, in fact a "constitutional" on the water.

The Superintendent of the Rhine and Rhone Canal was very civil, and endeavored to give me the information I required, but which he had not got, that is to say, the length, depth, and general character of the several rivers we proposed to navigate in connection with streams less "canalisés," so I had to start as usual, without any knowledge of the way.

With rather an ill-tempered "adieu" to Mulhouse, the Rob Roy set off again on her course, and the water assumed quite a new and unpleasant aspect, not that one *must* go by it, but it was not so much the water as the locks that were objectionable. For at each lock there is a certain form of operations to be gone through—all very trifling and without variety, yet requiring to be carefully performed, or you may have the boat injured, or a ducking for yourself.

When we come to a lock I have to draw to the bank, open my waterproof apron, put my package[1] and paddle ashore, then step out and haul the boat out of the water. By this time two or three persons usually congregate. I select the most likely one, and ask him to help in such a persuasive but dignified manner that he feels it is an honour to carry one end of the boat while I take the other, and so we put her in again above the barrier, and if the man looks poor, I give him some halfpence. At some of the locks they asked me for a "carte de permission," or "pass" for travelling on their canal, but I laughed the matter off, and when they pressed it with a "mais, monsieur!" I kept treating the proposal as a joke, until the officials were fairly baffled and gave in. We had in fact got into the canal as one gets over the hedge on to a public road, and as I did not use any of the water in the locks or any of the lock-keepers' time, and the "pass" was a mere form, price 5$d.$, it was but reasonable to go unquestioned; and beside, this "carte" could not be obtained except at the beginning of the whole canal.

How is it that the French, who are such slaves of rule and system in all their official life, are yet so violent in changes of their form of Government? and how is it that the Americans, who are so elastic in their regulations and so ready for novelty in action, are yet so pervasively consecutive in their form of Government?

Perhaps because the Yankee has the good sense to see that a Republic is the best or the only possible form for a new and huge body of people, which found itself suddenly without a dynastic head, and which could not wait in confusion through the long years of lineal authority which are absolutely necessary to establish a personal sovereign.

King-power in America would be as difficult to root as a Republic in France, and yet it would be easier for Americans to become monarchists than for Britons to become Republicans. But is there not a better reason for the success of America and the failure of France? that while France is all nerve and joints there is in her no national backbone of religion, whereas in America, though no man can claim majesty by birth, there is a true faith in God among the people, a fearless courage to confess it, and a widespread eagerness to serve with loyal devotion that One Eternal Sovereign Supreme.

After a time our route suddenly passed into the river Ill, a long dull stream, which flows through the Vosges into the Rhine. This water was now quite stagnant, and a mere collection of pools covered by thick scum. It was therefore a great comfort to have only a short voyage upon it. When the Rob Roy again entered the canal, an acquaintance was formed with a young lad, who was reading as he sauntered along. He was reading of canoe adventures in America, and so I got him to walk some miles beside me, and to help the boat over some locks, telling him he could thus see how different actual canoeing was from the book stories about it made up of romance! He was pining for some expansion of his sphere, and specially for foreign travel, and above all to see England.

We went to an *auberge*, where I treated my friend to a bottle of wine, its cost being twopence halfpenny. After he left, in the dark, I put my boat in a lock-keeper's house, and his son led me to the little village of Illfurth, a most unsophisticated place indeed, with a few vineyards on a hill behind it, though the railway has a station near. It was not easy to mistake which was the best house here even in the dark, so I inquired of Madame at "The White Horse" if she could give me a bed. "Not in a room for one alone; three others will be sleeping in the same chamber."

This she had answered after glancing at my puny package and travel-worn dress, but her ideas about the guest were enlarged when she heard how he had come, and so she managed (they always do if you give time and smiles and show sketches) to allot me a nice little room for myself with two beds of the hugest size, a water jug most minute, and sheets very coarse and clean. Another omelette was consumed while the customary visitors surrounded the benighted traveller; carters, porters, all of them with courteous manners, and behaving so well to me and to one another, and talking such good sense, as to make me feel how different from this is the noisy taproom of a roadside English "public."

Two fine fellows of the Gendarmerie came in for their penny half bottle of wine, and as both of them had been in the Crimea we had soon a most interesting conversation. This was conducted in French, but the people here usually speak a patois utterly impossible for any fellow to comprehend. In this jargon they were discussing me under various conjectures, and they settled at last that I must be rather an odd fish, but certainly "a gentleman," and probably "noble." They were most surprised to hear that I meant to stop all the next day at Illfurth, simply because it was Sunday, but they did not fail to ask for my passport, which until this time had been carried all the way without a single inquiry on the subject. The sudden change from a first-rate hotel this morning to the roadside inn at Illfurth was more entertaining on account of its variety than for its agreeableness; but in good health and good weather one can put up with anything.

The utter silence of peaceful and cool night in a place like this reigns undisturbed until about four o'clock in early morn, when the first sound is some matutinal cock, who crows first because he is proud of being first awake. After he has asserted his priority thus once or twice, another deeper toned rooster replies, and presently a dozen cocks are all in full song, and in different keys. In half an hour you hear a man's voice; next, some feminine voluble remarks; then a latch is moved and clicks, the dog gives a morning bark, and a horse stamps his foot in the stable because the flies begin to breakfast on his tender skin. At length a pig grunts, his gastric juice is fairly awake, and the day is begun. And so the stream of life, thawed from its sleep, flows gently on again, and at length the full tide of village business is soon in agitation, with men's faces and women's as full of grave import as if this French Stoke Pogis were the capital of the world.

While the inmates prepare for early mass, and my bowl of coffee is set before me, there are four dogs, eight cats, and seven canaries (I counted them) all looking on, moving, twittering, mewing, each evidently sensible that a being from some other land is present among them; and as these little pets look with doubtful inquiring eyes on the stranger, there is felt more strongly by him too, "Yes, I am abroad."

On Sunday I had a quiet rest, and walk, and reading, and then an Englishman, who had come out from Mulhouse to fish, dined in the pleasant arbour of the inn with his family. One of his girls managed to fall into a deep pond and was nearly drowned, but I heard her cries, and we soon put her to rights. This Briton himself spoke with quite a foreign accent, having been six years in France; but his Lancashire dialect reappeared in conversation, and he said he had just been reading about the canoe in a Manchester paper. His children had gone that morning to a Sunday school before they came out by railway to fish in the river here; but I could not help contrasting their rude north country manners with the good behavior of the little "lady and gentleman," children of my host. One of these, Philibert, was very intelligent, and spent an hour or two with me, so we became great friends. He asked all kinds of questions about England and America, and was delighted to receive a little book with a picture in it, to read it to his father, for it contained the remarkable conversation between Napoleon and his Marshal at St. Helena concerning the Christian religion, a paper well worth reading, whoever spoke the words.

This Sunday being an annual village fête, a band played, and some very uncouth couples waltzed the whole day. Large flocks of sheep, following their shepherds, wandered over the arid soil. The poor geese, too, were flapping their wings in vain as they tried to swim in water an inch deep, where usually there had been some pleasant pools in the river. I sympathized with the geese, for I missed my river sadly too. My bill here for two nights, with plenty to eat and drink, amounted to five shillings, and I left good Madame Nico with some regret, starting again on the canal, which looked more dull and dirty than before. After one or two locks this sort of travelling became so insufferable that I suddenly determined to change my plans entirely—for is not one free?

A few moments of thought, and I got on the bank to look for a way of deliverance. By the present route several days would be consumed in going over the hills over a series of tedious locks; and this very canal had been already traversed by the four-oar boat *Waterwitch* some years ago. Far off could be seen the vine-clad hills of the Vosges, and I decided at once to leave the canal, cross the country to those hills, cart the canoe over the range, and so reach the source of the Moselle, and thus begin to paddle on quite another set of rivers. We therefore turned the prow back, went down the canal, and again entered the river Ill, but soon found it was now too shallow to float even my canoe. Once more I retraced my way, ascending the locks, and passing by Illfurth, went on to reach a village where a cart could be had. Desperation made me paddle hard even in the fierce sun, but it was not that this so much troubled me as the humiliation of thus rowing back and forward for miles on a dirty, stagnant canal, and passing by the same locks two or three times, with the full conviction that the people who gazed at this procedure must believe me not only to be mad (this much one can put up with), but furiously insane, and dangerous to be at large.

Nobody likes to be stared at, and he must be bold indeed who can bear the sufferings of a martyr, without his cause or his glory. Ah, we are getting out of our depth, I fear, in metaphysics, which means, you know, "When ane maun explains till anither what he disna understaun himsel, that's metapheesics."

Well, when we came to the prescribed village, named Haidwiller, they had plenty of carts, but not one would come to help me even for a good round sum. It was their first day with the grapes, and "ancient customs must be observed;" so we went on still further to another village, where they were letting out the water from the canal to repair a lock.

Here was a position of unenviable repose for poor Rob Roy! No water to float in, and no cart to carry her. To aid deliberation I attacked a large cake of hot flour baked by the lock-keeper's dirty wife, and we stuck plums in it to make it go down, while the man hied off to the fields to get some animal that could drag a clumsy vehicle—cart is too fine a name for it—which I had impressed from a ploughman near.

The man came back leading a gloomy looking bullock, and we started with the boat now travelling on wheels, but at a most dignified pace. Our sketch opposite represents the lady cow which dragged the cart at Lauffenburg, but it will do almost equally well for the present equipage.

This was the arrangement till we reached another village, which had no vineyards, and where therefore we soon found a horse, instead of the gruff bullock; while the natives were lost in amazement to see a boat in a cart, and a foreigner in neutral tint gabbling beside it.

The sun was exceedingly hot, and the road was dusty; but the walk was a pleasant change, though my driver kept muttering to himself about my preference of foot pace to the fearful jolts of his cart.

We passed thus through several villages on a fine fruitful plain, and at some of them the horse had to bait, or the driver to lunch, or his employer to refresh the inner man, in every case the population being favoured with an account by the driver of all he knew about the boat, and a great deal more. At one of the inns on the road some new wine was placed on the table. It had been made only the day before, and its appearance was exactly like that of cold tea, with milk and sugar in it, while its taste was very luscious and sweet. This new wine is sometimes in request, but especially among the women. "Corn shall make the young men cheerful, and new wine the maids." (Zech. Ix. 17.)

NOTES

1 In the Baltic voyage the luggage was placed out of the way, forward, and the canoe being 20 lbs. Lighter than the old Rob Roy, many improvements were of course effected in passages of this sort. The invaluable "post office" waterproof bag of the Jordan cruise is the last improvement in this direction.

CHAPTER XII

River Thur—Fire! Fire!—Over the Vosges—"Th"—Popish Pilgrims—
Source of the Moselle—Remiremont—Launched on the Moselle—
Lovely Scenes—The Paddle—Spell-bound—Washerwomen—
Graceful Salute—Run away with—Policemen.

The little flag of the Rob Roy, which was always hoisted, even in a cart, showed signs of animation as evening came on, being revived by a fresh cool breeze from the beautiful Vosges mountains when we gradually brought their outline more distinctly near. Then we had to cross the river Thur, but that was an easy matter in these scorching days of drought. So the cavalcade went on till we drove the cart into the pretty town of Thann. The driver insisted on our going to *his* hotel, but I saw at once it could not be the best in the town of this size (for experience quickens perception in these matters), and I simply took the reins, backed out of the yard, and drove to a better one.

Here the hotel keeper had read of the Rob Roy, so it was received with all the honours, and the best of good things was at our disposal. In the evening I burned the magnesium lights as usual to amuse the rustics, who came in great crowds along the road, drawing home their bullock carts, loaded with large vats full of the new grapes, and singing hoarsely as they waved flowers and garlands aloft, and danced around them—the rude rejoicings for a bounteous vine harvest. It is remarkable how soon the good singing of Germany is missed when you cross into France, though the language of the peasant here was German enough and his sympathies too.

At night we went to see an experiment in putting out fires. A large bonfire was lighted in the marketplace, and the inventor of the new apparatus came forward, carrying on his back a vessel full of water, under the pressure of "six atmospheres" of carbonic acid gas. He directed this on the fire from a small squirt at the end of a tube, and it was certainly most successful in immediately extinguishing the flames.[1] This gentleman and other *savants* of the town then visited the boat, and the usual entertainment of the sketch book closed a pleasant day, which had begun with every appearance of being the reverse. Although this is a busy place, I found only one bookshop in it, and that a very bad one. A priest and two nuns were making purchases there, and I noticed that more images and pictures than printed books were kept for sale.

Next morning a new railroad enabled me to take the canoe a little further into the hills; but the officials fought hard to make her go separate, that is, in a "merchandise" train, though I said the boat was "my wife," and could not travel alone. At last they put their wise heads together, filled up five separate printed forms, charged double fare, and the whole thing cost me just ninepence. Verily, the French are still overloaded with forms, and are still in the straitwaistcoat of *système*.

The railway winds among green mountains, while here and there a "fabrik," or factory, nestles in a valley, or illumines a hillside at night with its numerous window lighted up. These are the chief *depôts* of that wonderful industry of taste which spreads the shawls and scarves of France before the eyes of an admiring world, for ladies to covet, and for their husbands to buy. It is said that the designs for patterns here cost large sums, as if they were the oil paintings of the first masters, and that three times as much is paid in France for cutting one pattern in wood as will be given by an English manufacturer.

At Wesserling we managed to mount the Rob Roy on a spring vehicle, and we set off gaily up the winding road that passes the watershed of the Vosges mountains. I never had a more charming drive. For six hours we were among woods, vineyards, bright rivulets, and rich pastures. Walking up a hill, we overtook a carriage, and found one of the occupants was an Englishman. But he had resided in France for more than twenty years, so really one could scarcely understand his English. He spoke of "dis ting," and "ve vill go," and frequently mingled French and German words with his native tongue. In a newspaper article here we noticed after the name "Matthews" the editor had considerately added, "pronounced in English, Massious." This was well enough for a Frenchman, but it was difficult to conceive how a real live Briton could fail in pronouncing "th." When he found out my name, he grasped my hand, and said how deeply interested he had been in a pamphlet written by one of the clan.[2]

The spring carriage had been chartered as an expensive luxury in this cheap tour, that is to say, my boat and myself were to be carried about thirty-five miles in a comfortable four-wheeled vehicle for twenty-six francs—not very dear when you consider that it saved a whole day's time to me and a whole day's jolting to the canoe, which seemed to enjoy its soft bed on the top of the cushion, and to appreciate very well the convenience of springs. After a good hard pull up a winding road we got to the top of the pass of this "little Switzerland," as it is called, and here was a tunnel on the very crest of the watershed. The arch of this dark tunnel as we passed through it made an excellent frame to a magnificent picture; broad France lay stretched before me. Every stream at our back went down to the all-absorbing Rhine, but those in front would wend their various ways, some to the Mediterranean, others into the Bay of Biscay, and the rest into the British Channel. A thousand peaks and wooded knolls were on this side and that, while a dim panorama of five or six villages and sunny plains extended in front. This was the chain of the Vosges mountains and their pleasant vales, where many valorous men have been reared. The most noted crusaders came from this district, from here the great Napoleon drew his best soldiers, and here there limped but lately the brave red-shirted Garibaldi.[3] Most of the community are Protestants.

High up on our left is a pilgrim station, where thousands of people come year by year, and probably they get fresh air and useful exercise. The French seem to walk farther for superstitious purposes than for exercise or amusement.[4]

Our English friend now got into my carriage, and we drove a little way from the road to the village of Bussang to see the source of the Moselle. This beautiful river rises under the "Ballon d'Alsace," a lofty mountain with a rounded top, and the stream consists at first of four or five very tiny trickling rivulets which unite and come forth in a little spring well about the size of a washing tub, from which the water flows across the road in a channel that you can bridge with your fingers. But this bubbling brook had great interest for me, as I meant to follow its growth until it would be strong enough to bear me on its cool, clear water, which as yet was only like feathers strewed among the grass, and singing its first music very pretty and low.

A romantic man must have piquant thought at the sight of a great river's source, and a poetic man must be stirred by its sentiment. Every great thought must also have had a source or germ, and it would be interesting to know how and when some of the grand ideas that have afterwards aroused nations first thrilled in the brain of a genius, a warrior, a philosopher, or a statesman. And besides having a source, each stream of thought had a current too, with ripples and deep pools, and scenery, as it were, around. Some thoughts are lofty, others broad; some are straight, and others round about; some are rushing, while others glide; only a few are both clear and deep.

But we are not to launch upon fancy's dreams, or to linger among the pretty valleys in the Vosges; and we go through these to find real water for the Rob Roy, and in this search we keep descending every hour. When the bright stars came out they glittered below thick trees in pools of the water now so quickly become a veritable river, and I scanned each lagoon in the darkness to know if it was still too small for the boat.

At Remiremont there was a bad sort of inn, where all was disorder and dirt. The driver sat down with me to a late supper, and behaved with true French politeness, which always shows better in company than in private, or when real self-denial or firm friendship is to be tested. So he ate of his five different courses, and had his wine, fruit, and neat little etceteras, and my bill next day for our united entertainment and lodging was just 3s. 4d. This *cocher* was an intelligent man, and conversed on his own range of subjects with considerable tact, and when our conversation was turned upon the greater things of another world he said, "They must be happy there, for none of them have ever come back"—a strange thought, oddly phrased. As he became interested in the subject, I gave him a paper upon it, which he at once commenced to read aloud.[5]

Next morning, the 20th of September, the Rob Roy was brought to the door in a handcart, and was soon attended by its usual levee; but as we had come into the town late at night the gazers were ignorant of any claims this canoe might have upon their respect, and some of them derided the idea of its being able to float the river here, or at any rate to go more than a mile or two. Having previously taken a long walk before breakfast to examine the Moselle, I was convinced that it could be begun even here and in this dry season. The porter was therefore ordered to advance, and the boat moved towards the river amid plaudits rather ambiguous, until a curious old gentleman, with green spectacles and a white hat, kindly brought the skeptical mob to their senses by telling them that he had read often about the boat, and they must not make fun of it now.

Then they all chopped round and changed their minds in a moment—the fickle French—and they helped me with a will, and carried the Rob Roy about a mile to the spot fixed upon for the start, which was speedily executed, with a loud and warm "Adieu!" and "Bon voyage!" from all.

It was pleasant again to grasp the paddle and to find clear water below, which we had not seen since the Danube, also a steady current, that was so much missed on the sluggish river Ill, and the Basel Canal. Pretty water flowers quivered in the ripples round the mossy stones, and park-like meadows sloped to the river with fruit trees heavy laden. After half an hour of congratulation that we had come to the Moselle rather than the Saone and the Doubs, I settled down to my work with gladness.

The water of this river was very clear and cool, meandering through long deep pools, and then over gurgling shallows; and the fish, waterfowl, woods, and lovely green fields were a most welcome change from the canal we had left. The sun was intensely hot, but the spare jib, as a shawl on my shoulders, defied its fierce rays, and so we glided along in solitary enjoyment. The numerous shallows required much activity with the paddle, and the Rob Roy had more bumps and thumps today than in any other day of the cruise. Of course I had often to get out and to tow her through the water: sometimes through the fields, or over rocks, but this was easily done with canvas shoes on, and flannel trousers made for constant ducking.

The aspect of the river had an unusual character for several miles, with low banks sloping backwards, and richly carpeted with grass, so that the view on either side was ample; while in front was a spacious picture of successive levels, seen to great advantage as the Rob Roy glided smoothly on crystal waters lipped with green. Again the playful river descends by sudden leaps and deep falls, chiefly artificial, and some trouble is caused in getting down each of these, for the boat had to be lowered by hand, with a good deal of gymnastic exercise among the slippery rocks, which were mantled by mosses and lichens that were studded in anything but botanical order.

The paddle now felt so natural in my hands from long use of it every day, that it was held unconsciously. In the beginning of my practice various tethers and ties were invented to secure this all-important piece of furniture from being lost if it should fall overboard, and I had practiced what ought to be done if the paddle should ever be beaten out of my hand by a wave, or dropped into the water in a moment of carelessness. But none of these plans were satisfactory in actual service. The strings got entangled when I jumped out suddenly, or I forgot the thing was tied when it had to be thrown out on the shore, so it was better to have the paddle perfectly loose and thus free, it never was dropped, even in those times of confusion when twenty things had to be done, and each to be done first, when an upset was imminent, and a jump out had to be managed instead.[6]

The movement of the paddle, then, became involuntary, just as the legs are moved in walking, and the ordinary difficulties of a river seemed to be understood by the mind without special observation, and to be dealt with naturally, without hesitation or reasoning as to what ought to be done. This faculty increased until long gazes upwards to the higher grounds or to the clouds above were fully indulged without apparently interrupting the steady and proper navigation of the boat, even when it was moving with speed.

On one of these occasions I had got into a train of thought on this subject, and was regretting that the course of the stream made me turn my back on the best scenery. I had spun round two or three times to feast my eyes upon some glowing peaks, lit up by the setting sun, until a sort of fascination, seized the mind, and a quiet lethargy crept over the system; and, moreover, a most illogical persuasion then settled that the boat always *did* go right, and that one need not be so much on the alert as to steer well. This notion still held me as we came into a cluster of a dozen rocks all dotted about, and with the stream welling over this one and rushing over that, and yet I was spellbound and doggedly did nothing to guide the boat's course. But the water was avenged on this foolish defiance of its power, for in a moment I was driven straight on a great rock, only two inches below the surface, and the boat at once swung round, broadside on the current, and then slowly but determinedly began to turn over. As it canted more and more my lax muscles were rudely aroused to action, for the plain fact stared out baldly that this stupid, lazy fit would end in a regular ducking.

The worst of it was I was not sitting erect, but stretched almost at full length in the boat, and one leg was entangled inside by the strap of my bag. In the moments following (that seem minutes in such case) a gush of thoughts went through the mind while the poor little boat was still turning over, until at last I gave a spring from my awkward position to jump into the water. The jerk released the canoe from the rock, but only the head and arms of its captain fell into the river—though in a most undignified *pose*, which was soon laughed off, when my seat was recovered, with a wet wig and dripping sleeves, which soon quite wakened and sobered me. So it was well to have done with sentiment and reveries, for the river was now quite in earnest about going along.

Permit me again to invite attention to the washerwoman; for this institution, which one does not find thus floating on our streams in England, becomes a very frequent object of interest if you canoe it on the Continent.

As the well in Eastern countries is the recognized place for gossiping, and in colder climes a good deal of politics is settled in the barber's shop, so here in fluvial districts the washing barge is the forum of feminine eloquence.

The respectability of a town as you approach it is shadowed forth by the size and ornaments of the *blanchiseusses'* float; and as there are often fifty faces seen at once, the type of female loveliness may be studied for a district at a time. While they wash they talk, and while they talk they thump and belabour the clothes; but there is always some idle eye wandering which speedily will catch sight of the Rob Roy canoe.

In smaller villages, and where there is no barge for them to use, the women have to do without one, and they kneel on the ground, so that even in far-off parts of the river we are sure to find them. A flat-sounding whack! whack! tells that round the corner we shall come upon at least a couple of washerwoman, homely dames, with brown faces and tall caps, who are wringing, slapping, and scrubbing the "linge." Though this may encourage the French cotton trade, I rejoice that my own shirts are of strong woolen stuff, which defies their buffeting.

I always fraternized with these ladies, doffing my hat, and drawing back my left foot for a bow, though graceful action was not observed under the macintosh. Other travellers, also, may find there is something to be seen and heard if they pass five minutes at the washing barge. But even if it were not instructive and amusing thus to study character when a whole group is met with at once, surely it is to be remembered that the pleasure of seeing a new sight and of hearing a foreigner speak cheerful and kind words is to many of these hard working, honest mothers a bright interlude in a life of toil.

To give pleasure is one of the best pleasures of a tourist; and it is in acting thus that the lone traveller feels no loneliness, while he pleases and is pleased. Two Englishmen may travel together agreeably among foreigners for a week without learning so much of the life, and mind, and manners of the people as will be learned in one day if each of the tourists goes alone, provided he is not too shy or too proud to open his eyes, and ears, and mouth among strangers, and if he has sense enough to be an exception to the rule that "Every Englishman is an island."

Merely for a change, I now ran the Rob Roy into a long millrace in search of breakfast. This stream having secured hold of the boat soon ran away with us stealthily in a winding course among the hayfields, and quite out of reach of the river, until it seemed that after all we were only in a streamlet for irrigation, which would vanish into rills an inch deep on it, and gravely and swiftly sped through the fields, and bestowed a nod now and then on the rural gazers. A fine boy of twelve years old soon trotted alongside, and I asked him if he was "an honest lad," which he answered by a blush, and "Yes." "Here is a franc, then. Go and buy me bread and wine, and meet me at the mill."

A few of the mill hands soon found out the canoe, which was moored, as I had thought, in quiet retirement, with its captain resting under a tree, and presently a whole crowd of them swarmed out, and shouted with delight as they pressed round to see. The boy brought a very large bottle of wine, and a loaf big enough to dine four men; and I set to work with a canoeist's appetite, and that happy *sang-froid* which no multitude of gazers could now disturb. Presently, one of the party invited me into her house, and soon set delicate viands before the new guest, while the others filled the room in an instant, and they were replaced by sets of fifty at a time, all very good humoured and respectful.

But it was so hot and bustling here that I resolved to go away and have a more pleasant and sulky meal by myself on some inaccessible island. The retreat through the crowd had to be regularly prepared for by military tactics; so I appointed four of the most troublesome boys as "policemen" to guard the boat in its transit across the fields, but they discharged their new duties with such vigour that two little fellows were soon knocked over into the canoe, and so we launched off, while the manager of the factory called in vain to his cotton spinners, who were all now in full cry after the boat, and were taking a holiday without leave.

As I trace these lines, written first in sunny laughing times of wayward France, it does indeed look as if her gloom of midnight had come at last as on a dark December day. Unhappy child of Europe, laughing, screaming, singing, raging, mountebank of the nations, scapegrace, and yet somehow the pet of us all, we are ashamed of you and yet proud of you—pretty, giddy France.

NOTES

1 This invention, l'Extincteur, has become well known in London, and it seems to be a valuable one.

2 The loss of the Kent East Indiaman by Fire in the Bay of Biscay, by General Sir D. MacGregor, K.C.B. (Religious Tract Society, Paternoster Row.) [Editor's note: MacGregor is referring here to his family "clan", not a member of the United States' right-wing extremists.)

3 The giant called "Anak," who was lately exhibited in London, came from the Vosges mountains.

4 Among other celebrated French "stations" there is the mountain of La Salette, near Grenoble, where, even in one day, 16,000 pilgrims

have ascended to visit the spot where the Virgin Mary was said to have spoken to some shepherds. On the occasion of my pilgrimage there I met some donkeys with panniers bringing down holy water (in lemonade bottles) which was sold throughout Europe for a shilling a bottle, until a priest at the bottom of the mountain started a private pump of his own. The woman who had been hired to personate the Holy Saint confessed the deception, and it was exploded before the courts of law in a report which I read on the spot; but the Roman Catholic papers, even in England, published attractive articles to support this flagrant imposture, and its truth and goodness were vehemently proclaimed in a book by the Romish Bishop of Birmingham, with the assent of the Pope.

Methinks it is easier to march barefoot 100 miles over sharp stones than to plod a true and honest walk of life on common pavement and with strong soled boots.

5 Some days previously a stranger gave me a bundle of papers to read, for which I thanked him much. Afterwards at leisure I examined the packet, which consisted of about thirty large pages sewn together, and comprising tracts upon politics, science, literature, and religion. The last subject was prominent, and was dealt with in a style clever, caustic, and censorious, which interested me much. These tracts were printed in England, and with good paper and type. They are a weekly series, distributed everywhere at six shillings a dozen, and each page is entitled "The Saturday Review."

6 After ten more voyages with precisely the same result, it may be stated that a spare paddle, so often recommended, would be quite superfluous. The bamboo mast was meant originally to serve also as a boat hook or hitcher, and had a ferrule and a fishing gaff neatly fastened on the end which went into the mast step. I recollect having used the boat hook *once* at Gravesend, but it was instantly seen to be a mistake. You don't want a boat hook when you canoe can come close alongside where it is deep, and will ground when it is shallow. Besides, to use a boat hook you must drop the paddle.

CHAPTER XIII

River Moselle—The Tramp—Battery of Blessings—
Halcyon—Painted Woman—Sad Loss—Very Shabby—
In a Hedge—A Discovery—River Meurthe—Flirting
—Ducks—A Moving House—A Mother's Tears
—Night Frolic—Salt Mine—Work for the Young

Under an arch of dark foliage, where the water was deep and still, I moored to the long grass, cast my tired limbs into the fantastic folds of ease, and, while the bottle lasted and the bread, I watched the bees and butterflies, and the beetles and the rats, and the coloured tribes of air and water life that one can see so well in a quiet half-hour like this.

How little we are taught at school about these wondrous communities, each with its laws and instincts, its beauties of form, and marvelous ingenuities! How little of flowers and insects, or of trees and animals, a boy learns as school lessons, while he is getting beaten into him at one end, and crammed in at the other, the complicated politics of heathen gods, and their impossible loves and faction fights.

The Moselle now rapidly enlarged in volume, though one could easily see that its stream had seldom been so low before. It is a very beautiful river to row on, especially in the higher waters. Then it winds to the west and north, and again, turning a little eastwards, it traverses a lovely country between Treves and Coblentz to join the ancient Rhine.

My resting place this evening was at Epinal, a town with little to interest; and so we could turn to books and pencils until it was time for bed. Next morning the scenery was by no means attractive, but there was plenty of hard work, which was enjoyed very much, my shoes and socks being off all day, for it was useless to put them on when so many occasions required me to jump out. Here was a plain country, with a gravel soil, and fast rushing of current; and then long pools like the Serpentine, and winding turns leading entirely round some central hill which the river insisted upon circumventing.

At noon we came upon a large number of labourers at work on a milldam, and as this sort of crowd generally betokens something to eat (always, at any rate, some drinkable fluid), I left my boat boldly in mid-stream, and knocked at a cottage, when an old woman came out.

"Madame, I am hungry, and you are precisely the lady who can make me an omelette."

"Sir, I have nothing to give you."

"Why," said I, "look at these hens; I am sure they have laid six eggs this morning, they seem so conceited."

She evidently thought I was a tramp demanding alms, and when told to look at the boat which had come from England, she said she was too old and too blind to see. However, we managed to make an omelette together, and she stood by (with an eye, perhaps, to her only fork) and chatted pleasantly, asking, "What have you got to sell?" I told her I had come there only for pleasure. "What sort of pleasure, Monsieur, can you possibly hope to find in *this* place?" But I was far too gallant to say bluntly that her particular mansion was not the ultimate object of the tour. After receiving a franc for the rough breakfast, she kept up a battery of blessings till the Rob Roy started, and she ended by shrieking out to a navvy looking on, "I tell you every Englishman is rich!"

Next day was bright and blue-skyed as before, and an early start found the fresh morning air on the river. Its name is sometimes pronounced "Moselle," and at other times "Mosel," what we should call "Mozle." When a Frenchman speaks of "la Moselle," he puts an equal amount of emphasis on each of the three syllables he is pronouncing; whereas we Englishmen call this river Mosélle. The name of a long river often goes through changes as it traverses various districts and dialects; for instance, the Missouri, which you hear travellers in Kansas call "Mzoory," while they wend along the Californian road.

When the scenery is tame to the canoeist, and the channel of the river is not made interesting by dangers to be avoided, then he can always turn again to the animals and birds, and in five minutes of watching he will surely see much to please. Here, for instance, we have the little kingfisher again, who had met us on the Danube and the Reuss, and whom we all know well in England; but now we are on a visit to his domain, and we see him in private alone. There are several varieties of this bird, and they differ in form and colour of plumage. This "Royal bird," the *Halcyon* of antiquity, the *Alcedo* in classic tongue, is called in German "Eisvogel," or "Ice bird," perhaps because he fishes even in winter's frost, or because his nest is like a bundle of icicles, being made of minnows' bones most curiously wrought together.

But now it is on a summer day, and he is perched on a twig within two inches of the water, and under the shade of a briar leaf, his little parasol. He is looking for fish, and is so steady that you may easily pass him without observing that gaudy back of azure, or the breast of blushing red.

When I desire to see these birds, I quietly move my boat till it grounds on a bank, and after it is stationary thus for a few minutes, the Halcyon fisher becomes quite unconcerned, and plies his pretty pranks as if unseen. He peers with knowing eye into the shallow below him, and now and then he dips his head a bit to make quite sure he has marked a fish worth seizing; then suddenly he darts down with a spluttering splash, and flies off with a little white minnow, or a struggling sticklebat nipped in his beak. If it is caught thus crosswise, the winged fisherman tosses his prey into the air, and nimbly catches it in his mouth, so that it may be gulped down properly. Then he quivers and shakes with satisfaction, and quickly speeds him to another perch, flitting by you with wonderful swiftness, as if a sapphire had been flung athwart the sunbeam, flashing beauteous colours in its flight.

Or, if bedtime has come, or he is fetching home the family dinner, he flutters on and on, and then with a sharp little note of "good-bye" he pops into a hole, the dark staircase to his tiny nest, and there he finds Mrs. Halcyon sitting in state, and thirteen baby kingfishers gaping for the dainty fish. This pretty bird has an air of quaint mystery, soft beauty, and vivid motion, all combined, which has made him a favourite with the Rob Roy, and often we have paddled beside him on the deep jungle banks of Jordan.

Strangely enough, the Moselle in this part of its course actually gets less and less as you descend it. Every few miles some of the water is drawn off by a small canal to irrigate the neighbouring land, and in a season of drought like this very little of the abstracted part returns. They told me that the river never has been so "basse" for thirty, and I was therefore an unlucky *voyageur* in having to do for the first time what could have been done more easily in any other season.

As evening fell we reached the town of Chatel, and the Rob

Roy was sent to bed in the washhouse of the hotel. But five minutes had not elapsed before a string of visitors came for the usual inspection of the boat. While I sauntered along the bridge a sprightly youth came up, who had not seen the canoe, but who knew I was "one of her crew." He was most enthusiastic on the subject, and took me to see *his* boat, a ghastly looking flat-bottomed open cot, painted all manner of patterns; and as he was extremely proud of her, I did not tell him that a boat is like a woman, too good for paint, which spoils a pretty one, and makes a plain one hideous.

Then he came for a look at the Rob Roy, and, poor fellow, it was amusing to observe how instantly his countenance fell from pride to envy. He had a "boating mind," but he had never seen a really pretty boat till now. However, to console himself he invited me to another hotel to drink success to the canoe in Bavarian beer, and to see my drawings, and then I found that my intelligent, eager, and, we may add, gentlemanly friend was the waiter there!

A melancholy sensation pervaded the Rob Roy today, in consequence of a sad event, the loss of the captain's knife. We had three knives on board starting from England: one had been already given away in reward for some signal service, another was lost, and no wonder—in so many leaps and somersaults. The canoeman should have his boat knife secured to a lanyard.

A singular conformation of the river bed was observed upon this part of the Moselle. Without much warning the banks of rock became quite vertical and narrowed close together. They reminded me of the rock cutting near Liverpool, on the old railway to Manchester. The stream there was very deep, but its bed was full of enormous stones and crags, very sharp and jagged, which, however, could be easily avoided, because the current was gentle.

A man I found fishing told me that a little further on

there was an "impossible" place, so when after half a mile the well-known sound of rushing waters came, we beat to quarters and prepared for action. The ribbon to keep my hat was tied down. Sleeves and trousers were tucked up. The apron was braced tight, and the baggage secured below; and then came the eager pleasures of wishing, hoping, expecting, fearing—those mingled elements of what we call "excitement."

Very soon the river itself took a very strange form. If you suppose a trench cut along Oxford Street to get at the gas pipes, and if all the water of a river which had filled the street before were to suddenly disappear in the trench, that would be exactly what the Moselle had become.

The plateau of rock on each side was perfectly dry, though in flood times, no doubt, the river covers that too. The river boiled and foamed through this channel from three to twenty feet deep, but only in the trench, which was not five feet wide. An intelligent man came near to see me enter this curious passage, but when we had gone a little way I had to stop the boat, by putting my hands on both sides of the river! Then I debarked and carefully let the boat drive along the current, but still held by the painter. Soon the current was too narrow and fast even for this process, so I pulled the canoe upon the dry rock, and sat down to breathe and to cool my panting frame. Two other gentlemen had come near me by this time, and on a bridge above them were several more with ladies. I had to drag the boat some hundred yards over most awkward rocks, and these men hovered round and admired, and even talked to me, and actually praised my perseverance, yet not one offer of any help did any one of them give!

In deep water again, and now exactly under the bridge I looked up and found the whole party regarding the Rob

Roy with curiosity and smiles. Within a few yards was a large house that these people had come from, and I thought their smiles were surely to preface, "Would you not like a glass of wine, Sir, after your hour of hard work?" But as it meant nothing of the sort I could not help answering their united adieux! by these words, "Adieu, ladies and gentlemen. Many to look, but none to help. The exhibition is gratuitous!" Was it rude to say this? I couldn't help thinking it.

One or two other places gave trouble without interest, such as when we had to push the boat into a hedge point foremost, and to pull it through by main force from the other side, and then, after all, we had pushed her into the wrong field, so the operation had to be done over again in a reverse direction. But all this counted in the day's work, and it was forgotten after a good sleep, or was recompensed by some interesting adventure. The water of the Moselle is so clear that the scenery under the surface continually occupied my attention. In one long reach, unusually deep and quiet, and shallow, because of the long drought, I was gazing down at some huge trout, when a large stone, the upper part of a fine column, was suddenly perceived at the bottom, at least ten feet below me. The capital showed it to be Ionic, and near this was another, a broken pediment of large dimensions, and a little further on a pedestal of white marble. I carefully examined both banks, to see if a Roman villa or bridge, or other ruin, indicated how these subaqueous relics had come into this strange position, and I inquired diligently at Charmes, the next town; but although much curiosity was shown on the subject, no information was obtained, except that the Romans had built a fort somewhere on the river (but plainly not at that spot), so we may consider that the casual glance at the fish revealed a curious fragment of the past hitherto probably unnoticed, and that these carved pillars may have been upset in this pool many centuries ago.

After paddling along the Moselle, from as near to its source as my canoe could find water, until the scenery became dull at Charmes, we bid farewell to this beauteous stream, which in years since then has had its waters burdened with corpses and fouled by the carrion of ten thousand chargers—starved or slain.

It was resolved to go next to Blainville, on the river Meurthe, which is a tributary of the Moselle, for I thought some new scenery might be found in this direction. The Rob Roy was therefore sent by herself in a goods' train, the first separation between us for three months. It seemed as if the little boat, leaning on its side in the truck, turned from me reproachfully, and we foreboded all sorts of accidents to its delicate frame, but the only thing lost was a sponge, a necessary appendage to a boat's outfit when you desire to keep it perfectly dry and clean, and an article frequently stolen afterwards in my Baltic cruise.

Two railway porters, with much good-humoured laughing, carried the Rob Roy from the station to the water, and again we paddled cheerily on a new river, with scenery and character quite different from the Moselle. The Meurthe winds through rich plains of soft earth, with few rocks and little gravel. But then in its shallows it has long thick mossy weeds, all under the surface. These were found to be very troublesome, because they got entangled with my paddle, and since they could not be seen beforehand, the best channel was not discernible, as it is where rocks or gravel give those various forms of ripples which the captain of a canoe soon learns to scan like a chart telling the depth in inches. Moreover, when you get grounded among these long weeds, all pointed down stream, it is very difficult to back out, for it is then like combing your hair against the grain.

The larger rivers in France are all thoroughly fished. In every nook you find a fisherman. They are just as numerous here as they are rare in Germany. And yet one would think that fishing is surely more adapted to the contemplative German than to the vivacious French. Yet, here they are in France by hundreds, both men and women, and every day, each staring intently on a tiny float, or at the grasshopper bait, and he is quite satisfied if now and then he can pull up a fish the size of your thumb. Not one of these fishers I spoke to had ever seen an artificial fly.

Generally, these people are alone, and when they asked me at hotels if I did not feel lonely in the canoe, the answer was, "Look at your fishermen, for hours by choice alone. They have something to occupy attention every moment, and so have I." Sometimes, however, there is a whole party in one clumsy boat. The *pater familias* sits content, and recks not if all his time is spent baiting his line and lighting his pipe. The lazy "hopeful" lies at full length on the grass, while a younger brother strains every nerve to hook a knowing fish that is laughing at him under water, and winking its pale eye to see the fisher just toppling over. Mademoiselle chatters whether there are bites or not, and another, the fair cousin, has got on shore, where she can bait her hook and set her cap and simper to the bold admirer by her side.

Then besides, we have the fishers with nets. These are generally three men in a boat, with its stem and its stern cocked up, and the whole affair looking as if it must be upset. Exactly such boats were painted by Raphael in the great Cartoons, where it may be observed how small the boat is when compared with the men it carries.

Again, there are some young lads searching under the stones for *ecrevisses*, the freshwater prawns so much in request, but which give very little food for a great deal of trouble. Near these fishers the pike plies his busy sportsman's life below the surface, and sometimes a poor little trout would leap high into the air to escape from the long-nosed pursuer, who followed him even out of the water, and snapped his jaws on the sweet morsel impudently. This sound, added to the very suspicious appearance of the Rob Roy gliding among the islands; decides the doubtful point with a duck, the leader of a flock of wild ducks that have been swimming down stream in front of me with a quick glance on each side, every one of them seemingly indignant at this intrusion on their haunts. At last they find it really will not do, so with a scream and a spring they flap the water and rise in a body to seek if there be not elsewhere at least some one nook to nestle in where John Bull does not come.

That bell you hear tinkling is at the ferry, to call the ferryman who lives at the other side, and he will jump into his clumsy boat, which is tied to a pulley running across the river. He has only to put his oar aslant and the current soon brings the boat to the other bank. Paddling on further, after a chat with the ferryman (he is sure to be ready for that), a phenomenon appears. We see a house, large, new, and of two stories high—it has actually moved. We noticed it a few minutes ago, and now it has changed it position. While we gaze in astonishment, lo! the whole house entirely disappears. Now the true explanation of this is soon found when we get round the next corner of the reach—the house is a great wooden bathing "établissement," built on a barge, and it is being slowly dragged up the stream.

After wonder comes sentiment. Three women are seen on the riverbank evidently in great alarm: a mother, a daughter, and a servant-maid, who are searching in vain for two boys, supposed to have gone away to fish, but now missing for many hours. The ladies eagerly inquired if I had seen the lads, and implored me with tears to give them advice. I tried my best to recollect, but no! I had not seen the boys, and so the women went away distracted, and left me sorrowful—who would not be so at a woman's tears, a mother's too? But suddenly, when toiling in the middle of a difficult piece of rock work, I remembered having seen those very boys, so I ran over the fields after the anxious mamma and soon assured her that the children had been safe an hour ago, and their faithful servant with them, but that *he* had become the fisherman, and they, like boys, had soon tired of the rod, and were playing with a goat. When the poor mother heard that the little fellows were safe, her tears of joy were quite affecting, and they vividly recalled one's schoolboy days, when the thoughtless playtime of childhood so often entails anxiety on a loving mother's heart. Such, then, are the river sights and river wonders, new, though perhaps trifling, but far more lively and entertaining than the common incidents of a dusty road, or a whirring, shrieking train.

With a few wadings and bumpings, and one or two "vannes," or weirs, we slipped along pleasantly until evening came. Still it was only a slow stream, and the towers of St. Nicholas, long visible on the horizon, seemed ever to move from side to side without being any nearer, so much does this river wind in its course. The Rob Roy paddled at her best pace, but the evening rapidly grew darker, until we overtook two youths in a boat, the first time we had noticed Frenchmen rowing for exercise. They could not keep up with the canoe, so I had to leave them ingloriously aground on a bank, and yet they were too lazy to get out and help their boat over the difficulty.

Next there was a great weir about fifteen feet in height, the deepest we had encountered, and half a sigh was heaved that there was no escape from the bother of getting out and gymnasticizing here after a long day's work to get the boat over this weir in the dark; and then, what was far worse, I found myself in a maze of shallows, without any light to see how to get through them. Whenever I stopped for a rest, there was only darkness, silence, and no motion—not even the excitement of a current too arouse. Finally, I had to wade and haul the boat along, and jump in and ferry myself over the pools, for nearly half a mile, until at length the "lookout" man of our starboard watch hailed loudly, "A bridge and a house on the lee bow!" and a joyous cheer burst forth from the crew. All this, which may be told in a few lines, took a full hour of very tiresome work, though, as there was no current, there was no danger, and it was merely tedious, wet, unlighted, and uncomfortable, so I sang and whistled all the time.

When the bridge was reached of course there must be a town, and then happened a scene almost an exact counterpart of that which took place at Gegglingen, on the Danube. For when after hauling up my boat on the dark shore, and all dripping wet, I mounted to the house above, and aroused the inmates—a window opened, and a worthy couple appeared in their nightdresses, holding a candle to examine the intruder. The tableau was most comical. The man asked, "Is it a farce?" He could scarcely expect a traveller from England to arrive there at such an hour. But he soon helped me to carry the boat to a little Restaurant, where a dozen men were drinking, who rushed out with lamps to look at the boat, and we had to carry her through the dark streets to another house, where another lot of topers received me in like style. We put the Rob Roy into a garden here, and her sails flapped next morning while a crowd gazed over the walls with anxious curiosity. The husband, who had thus left his sleeping spouse that he might carry my wet boat, was highly pleased with a five-franc piece, which must have been like a five-pound note to him in such a cheap country. Next morning we surveyed the scene of last night's adventure, and it was very amusing to trace the various channels we had groped about in during black darkness.

Here I met a French gentleman of gay and pleasant manner, but who bemoaned his lot as Secretary of a great factory in this outlandish place, instead of being in joyous, thoughtless, brilliant Paris, where, he said, often for days together he never slept in a bed but ran one night into the next by balls, theatres, and parties. He kindly took me to see the great salt works, which send refined salt throughout Europe. This rock salt is hoisted out of a deep mine in blocks like those of coal, having been hewn from the strata below, which are pierced by long and lofty galleries. Then it is covered in tanks by water, which becomes saturated, and is conducted to flat evaporating pans, when the water is expelled by the heat of a furnace, and the salt dries in masses like snowdrift. Salt that is sold by weight they judiciously wet again, and other qualities sold by measure they cleverly deposit in crooked crystals, so as to take up as much space as possible!

We found a canal here, and the river was so shallow the Rob Roy mounted to the artificial channel, and with a strong and fair wind she was soon sailing along. This canal has plenty of traffic upon it, and only a few locks; so it was by no means tedious. They asked for my card of permission, but I smiled the matter off as before. However, an officer of the canal who was walking alongside looked much more seriously at the infringement of rules, and when we came to a lock he insisted we must produce the "carte." As a last resort, I showed him the well worn sketch book, and then he at once gave in. In fact, after he had laughed at a culprit's caricatures, how could he gravely sentence him to penalties?

It is wonderful how a few lines of drawing will please these outlying country people. Sometimes we gave a small sketch to a man when it was desirable to get rid of him: he was sure to take it away to show outside, and when he returned we had gone. Once I gave to a little girl a portrait of her brother, and next morning she brought it again all crumpled up. Her mother said that the child had held it all night in her hand.

Work you the young, O brother canoemen. Get the "Boy's Beadle" to befriend the hapless wanderers. Teach them to earn their bread and not to beg. Change their sodden brown rags into bright red coats, as shoeblacks, or bright blue jackets, as sailor boys, and hurrah for the "Chichester," the floating home of the homeless boy. Teach him to read, and give him a "British Workman," and a "Boy's Own Paper," and

"Home Words," and a "Chatterbox," and tear up the journals of garbage.

Sit steady on the "School Board," Rob Roy, as you have sat on the foot board of your canoe.

Pray for them all, these little folk, or your work will be lifeless. Don't mind the "cant" of the people who call it "cant" to kneel while you work. A Strong Arm was reached far down to save you and me, and the boy and the girl, that cry to us both in their misery.

CHAPTER XIV

Luxuries—Monks—Camp at Chalons—Inns of Court—A Widower—
Leaks—Come to see a Smash—Champagne—The River Marne—
Name of my Wife—Silence—The Sun—Rafts and Flocks—
Newspapers—Millstones—Hot Wind—Old Soldier

The canal brought me to Nancy, a fine old town, with an Archbishop, a Fieldmarshal, a good hotel, large washhand basins, drums, bugles, ices, and all the other luxuries of life. Yet Nancy surrendered all these to the summons of Uhlans! In the cathedral there was more tawdry show about the Mass than we ever remarked before, even in Italy. At least thirty celebrants acted in the performance, and the bowings and turnings and grimaces of sedate old men clad in gorgeous dirty needlework, fumbling with trifles and muttering Latin, really passed all bounds: they were an insult to the population, who are required to attend this vicarious worship, and to accept such absurdities as the true interpretation of "This do in remembrance of Me."

A large congregation, nearly all women, listened to an eloquent sermon from a young priest who glorified an old saint. It is possible that the ancient worthy was a most respectable monk, but probably a good deal like the monks one meets now in the monasteries, and having lived pretty frequently with these gentlemen in Europe, Asia, and Africa, one smiles to think of canonizing such folk as if any one of them had unapproachable excellence. Perhaps, however, this particular monk distinguished himself by proper daily ablutions, and so gained the rare reputation of being reasonably clean. In the afternoon the relics of the monk were borne through the streets by a procession of some thousand women and a few men. These ladies, some hundreds of whom were dressed in white muslin, chanted as they slowly marched, and all the bystanders took off their hats, but I really could not see what adoration was due to the mouldering bones of a withered friar, so my excellent straw hat was kept on my head.

    The French, who live in public, must have a public religion, a gregarious worship, with demonstrative action and colours and sounds. Deep devotion, silent in its depth, is for the north and not for this radiant sun, though you will find that quieter worship again in lower latitudes where the very heat precludes activity. Some thirty years ago, one of our ablest Cambridge men read a paper on the influence of the insular position and the climate of Britain upon our national character. For the Frenchman, in a third-rate town like Nancy, for instance, nearly all the *agrements* depend on the climate, and they would be sadly curtailed by rain or snow. So when this Frenchman visits England and gets laughed at for mistakes in our difficult language, and has to eat only two dishes for dinner, and drinks bad coffee, and has no evening lounge in the open air, and is then told to look at our domestic life and finds he cannot get an entrance there (for how very few French do enter there), his miseries are directly caused by our climate, and no wonder his impression of Albion is that we are all fog and cotton and smoke, and everything *triste*.

From Nancy the canoe went by rail to meet me on the river Marne, and while the slow luggage train lumbered along I went off to visit the Camp of Chalons, the Aldershot of France. An omnibus takes you from the railway station, by a long straggling street of very little houses, built badly, and looking as if one and all could be pushed down by your hand. These are not the military quarters, but the self-grown parasite sutlers' town, which springs up near every camp. Here is "Place Solferino," and there you see "Rue Malakhoff," where the sign of the inn is a Chinaman having his pigtail lopped off by a Français. The camp is in the middle of a very large plain, with plenty of dust and white earth, which glared on my eyes intensely, this being the hottest day during the cruise. But there are trees for shade, and a good deal of grass on these extensive downs, where great armies manœuvred to march past the late Emperor enthroned under a bower on that hill crest overlooking all—and then soon fled in terror.

The permanent quarters for the troops consist of about 500 separate houses, substantial, airy, and well lighted, all built of brick and slated, and kept in good repair; each of these is about seventy feet long, twenty broad, and of one story high. A million and a half pounds sterling have already been expended on this camp. Behind the quarters are the soldiers' gardens, a feature added lately to the camps in England. There were only a few thousand soldiers at the place, so we soon saw all that was interesting, and then at a restaurant I observed about twenty officers go to breakfast together, but their loud, coarse, and outrageously violent conversation really amazed me. The din was monstrous and without intermission. We had never before fallen in with so very bad a specimen of French manners, and I cannot help thinking that there may have been special reasons why these men went on bellowing for half an hour as they ate their breakfast.

The military mess system has been tried in the French army several times, but it always fails, as the French Clubs do, on the whole. It is not wise, however, for a traveller to generalize too rapidly upon the character of any portion of a great people if he has not lived long among them. By a hasty glance you may discern that a stranger has a long nose, but you must have better acquaintance with him before you can tell his character.[1]

Another interesting town in this department of France is Rheims (spelt Reims, and pronounced very nearly Rens). I enjoyed a visit to its very splendid cathedral, which is one of the finest in Europe, very old, very large, very rich, and celebrated as the place of coronation for the French sovereigns. Besides all this it is kept in good order, and is remarkably clean. The outside is covered with stone figures, most of them rude in art, but giving at a distance an appearance of prodigal richness of material.

A little periodical called *France Illustrated* is published at fourpence each number, with a map of the Department, several woodcuts of notable places or events, and a brief history of the principal towns, concluding with a *résumé* of the statistics of the Department. A publication of this kind would be very useful in England; and for travellers especially, who could purchase at the County town the particular number then required. In one of the adjoining Departments, this publication said that there are about a hundred suicides in the year among a population of half a million. Surely this is an alarming proportion; and what should we say if Manchester had to report that a hundred men and women in one year put themselves to death?

But we are subsiding, you see, into the ordinary tales of

a traveller, because I am waiting now for the train and the Rob Roy, and certainly this my only experience of widowerhood made me long again for the well-known yellow oaken side of the boat and her pink-brown cedar deck. Well, next morning is the canoe at Epernay, arrived all safe at a cost of 2s. 6d. All safe we thought at first, but we soon found she had been sadly bruised, and would surely leak. On the railway platform in the hot sun, we occupied three good hours in making repairs and greasing the seams. But after all this trouble, when we put the boat into the Marne, the water oozed in all round.

It is humiliating to sit in a leaky boat—it is like using a lame horse or a crooked gun; of the many needful qualities of a boat the first is to be staunch. So I stopped at the first village, and got a man to mix white lead and other things, and worked this into the seams, leaving it to harden while I fed in the auberge by the shore, where they are making the long rafts to go down to Paris, and where hot farmers sip their twopenny bottle of wine.

The raft man was wonderfully proud of his performance with the canoe, and he called out to each of his friends as they walked past, to give them its long history in short words. When he was paid at last, he said I must never forget that the canoe had been thoroughly mended in the middle of France, at the village of——, but I really do not remember the name. However, there were not wanting tests of his workmanship, for the Rob Roy had to be pulled over many dykes and barriers on the Marne. Some of these were of a peculiar and novel construction. A "barrage" reached across the stream, and there were three steps or falls on it, with a plateau below each. The water ran over these steps, and was sometimes only a few inches in depth on the crest of each fall, where it had to descend about eight inches. This, of course, would have been easy enough for the canoe to pass, but then a line of iron posts was ranged along each plateau, with chains tied from the top of one post to the bottom of another, diagonally, a very puzzling arrangement to steer through in a fast current.

In cases of this sort we usually went ashore to reconnoitre, and having calculated the angle at which we must enter the passage obliquely (down a fall, and across its stream), I managed to get successfully through several of these strange barriers. But we came at length to one which was extremely difficult, because the chains were slack, and there was only an inch or two of "law" on either side of the channel through them. Just then a man happened to see my movements, and he called some dozen of his fellow navvies from their work to look at the navigator. The captain of the canoe was therefore incited to try the passage, and he resolved to be at any rate cool and placid, however much discomfiture was to be endured. The boat was steered to the very best of my power, but her bow swerved an inch in the swift oblique descent, and instantly it was locked in the chains, while I quietly stepped out (whistling in air in slow time), and steadily lifted the boat through the iron network and got into her, dripping wet, though wincing not. The navvies cheered a long and loud bravo! But the canoeist felt ashamed of having yielded to the desire for ignorant applause, and round the nest corner he changed his wet things, a wiser and a sadder, but dry.

This part of the river is in the heart of champagne country, and all the softly swelling hills around are thickly covered by vineyards. The vine for champagne is exceeding small, and grows round one stick, so the hillside looks just like a carding brush, from the millions of these little sharp-pointed rods upright in the ground and close together, without any fence between the innumerable lots. The grape for champagne is always red, and never white (so they said), though white grapes are grown for eating. During the last two months few people had consumed more grapes in this manner than the chief mate of the Rob Roy.

On one of these hills we noticed the house of Madame Clicquot, whose name has graced many a cork of champagne bottles and of bottles not champagne. The vineyards of Ai, near Epernay, are the most celebrated for their wine. After the bottles are filled, they are placed neck downwards, and the sediment collects near the cork. Each bottle is then partly uncorked for an instant in this position, and the confined gas forces out a little of the wine with the sediment, while a skilful man replaces the cork. When the bottles are stored in "caves," or vast cellars, the least change of temperature causes them to burst by hundreds. Sometimes one-fourth of the bottles explode in this manner, and it is said that the renowned Madame Clicquot lost 400,000 bottles in the hot autumn of 1843, before sufficient ice could be fetched from Paris to cool her spacious cellars. Every year about fifty million bottles of genuine champagne are made in France, and no one can say how many more millions of bottles of "French champagne" are imbibed every year by a confiding world. Even Bellona respects these bottles.

The Marne is a large and deep river, and its waters are kept up by barriers every few miles. It is rather troublesome to pass these by taking the boat out and letting it down on the other side, and in crossing one of them the stern of the canoe had a serious blow against an iron bar. This collision started four planks from the sternpost, and revealed to me also that the whole frame had suffered from the journey that night on an open truck. But, as my ship's carpenter was on board, and had nails and screws, we soon managed to make all tight again,[2] and by moonlight came to Dormans, where she had the invariable run of visitors, until everybody went to bed.

It was curious to remark the different names by which the canoe was called, and among these were the following: "*Bateau*", "*schiff*", "*bôt*", "*barca*", "*canôt*", "*caique*" (the soldiers who have been in the Crimea call it thus), "*chaloupe*", "*navire*", "*schipp*" (Low German), "*yacht*" ("jacht"—Danish, "jaht," from "jagen," to ride quickly—properly a boat drawn by horses). Several people have spoken of it as "*bateau à vapeur*," for in the centre of France they have never seen a steamboat, but the usual name with the common people is "*petit bateau*," and among the educated people "*nacelle*" or "*périssoir*," this last as we call a dangerous boat a "coffin" or "sudden death." The paddler is "*pagayeur*." In the East the Turks and Egyptians called her "*shaktoora*," and sometimes "*sheitan*" (spirit).

An early start next morning found us slipping along with a tolerable current and sailing before a fine fresh breeze, but under the same blue sky. I had several interesting conversations with farmers and others riding to market along the road which here skirts the river. What most surprises the Frenchman is that a traveller can possibly be happy alone! However selfish it may seem to be, it is far best for this sort of journey to travel entirely *seul*.

Pleasant trees and pretty gardens are here on every side in plenty, but where are the houses of the gentlemen of France, and where are the French gentlemen themselves? This is a difference between France and England which cannot fail to "knock" the observant traveller (as Artemus Ward would have said)—the notable absence of country seats during hours and hours of passage along the best routes; whereas in England the prospect from almost every hill or woodland would have a great house at the end of its vista, and the environs of every town would stretch into outworks of villas smiling in the sun. The French have ways and fashions which are not ours, but their nation is large enough to entitle them to a standard of their own, just as the Americans, with so great a people agreed on the matter, may surely claim liberty to speak with a twang, and to write of a "plow."

It is a mistake to say that we Britons are a silent people compared with the French or Americans. At some hundred sittings of the table d'hôte in both these countries I have found more of dull, dead silence than in England at our inns. An Englishman accustomed only to the domestic chat of a pleasant dinner feels ill at ease, perhaps, when dining with foreigners, and so he notices their silence all the more; but the purely French table d'hôte (not in the big barrack hotel, for English tourists) has as little general conversation as any dinner in England, and an American table has far less.

Here in France come six or seven middle-class men to dine. There is the napkin kept for each from yesterday, and recognized by the knots he tied on it. He puts it up to his chin like the pinafore of a baby, and wipes plate, fork, and spoon with the other end, and eats bits and scraps of many dishes, and scrapes his plate almost clean, and then departs, and not one word has been uttered all the time.

Again, there is the vaunted French climate. Bright sun, no doubt, but pray forget not that it is so very bright as to compel all rooms to be darkened from ten till four every day. At noon the town is like a cemetery; no one thinks of walking, riding, or looking out of his window in the heat. From seven to nine in the morning, and from an hour before sunset to any time you please at night, the open air is delicious. But in a week of our common summer weather we see more of the sun in England than in France, for we seldom have so much of it at once as to compel us for six hours to close our eyes against its fierce rays. In fact, the sensation of life in the South, after eleven o'clock in the morning, is that of *waiting for the cool hours*, and so day after day is a continual reaching forward to something about to come; whereas, an English day of sunshine is an enjoyable present from beginning to end. Once more, let it be remembered that twilight lasts only for half an hour in the sunny South; that delicious season of musing and long shadows is a characteristic of the northern latitudes which very few Southerners have ever experienced at all.

The run down the Marne for about 200 miles was a pleasant part of the voyage, but not so exciting in adventure as the paddling on unknown waters. Long days of work could therefore be now well endured, for constant exercise had trained the body, and the Rob Roy's paddle was in my hands for ten hours at a time without weariness, and sometimes even for twelve hours at a stretch.

After a comfortable night at Chateau Thierry in the Elephant Hotel, which is close to the water, I lowered my canoe from a hayloft into the river. The current gradually increased, and the vineyards gave place to forest trees. See, there are the rafts, some made of casks, lashed together with osiers, some made of planks, others of hewn logs, and others of great rough trees. The straw hut on each is for the captain's cabin, and the crew will have a stiff fortnight's work to drag, push, and steer this congeries of wood on its way to the Seine. The labour spent merely in adjusting and securing the parts is enormous, but labour of that kind costs little here.

Further on there is a large flock of sheep led to the river to drink, in the orthodox pastoral manner of picture-books, but also driven by the sagacious shepherd's dogs, who seem to know perfectly that the woolly multitude has come precisely to drink, and, therefore, the dogs cleverly press forward each particular sheep, until it has got a place by the cool brink of the water. In the next quiet bay a village maid drives her cow to the river, and chats across the water with another, also leading in a cow to wade knee deep, and to dip its broad nose, and lift it gently again from the cool stream. On the road alongside is a funny little waggon, and a whole family are within. This concern is actually drawn along by a goat. Its little kid skips about, for the time of toil has not yet come to the youngling, and it had better gambol now.

But here is the bridge of Nogent, so I leave my boat in charge of an old man, and give positive pleasure to the cook at the auberge by ordering a breakfast. Saints' portraits adorn the walls, and a "sampler" which some little girl had worked, with only twenty-five letters in the alphabet, when the "w" was as yet ignored in classic French grammars, though it has now to be constantly used in their common books and newspapers. Why, they even adopt our sporting terms, and you see in a paper that such a race was only "un Walkover," and that another was likely to be "un dead heat."

And then these French newspapers, what poor weaklings they are at best, with each writer's signature stripping him of his best title, the anonymous, like an actor off the boards, or a fiddler in a frock coat.

Perish that flimsy page with its "chocolat" and lotteries in huge letters, and its novelette at the end! and oh! for the goodly "Times," and the dapper "News," and the ample "Standard," and the blithe "Spectator," and the Saturday Satire, and the "thirteenth 'dishun of the 'Echo'." Is it a very naughty thing to smile this evening in the face of that man who has set the world to rights today by that scarifying leader he wrote last night?

Suddenly in my quiet paddling here the sky was shaded, and on looking up amazed I found a cloud; at last, after six weeks of brilliant blue and scorching glare, one fold of the fleecy curtain has been drawn over the sun. The immediate effect of this cooler sky was very invigorating, and yet after hot glare so long beating from above, and reflected upwards into my face from the water, it seemed the most natural thing to be always in a blaze of light, though much of the inconvenience of it was avoided by a plan which is explained in the Appendix, with some other hints to Boating Men. The day went pleasant now, and with only the events of ordinary times, which need not be recounted. The stream was steady, the banks were people, and many a blue-bloused countryman stopped to look at the canoe as she glided past, with the captain's socks and canvas shoes on the deck behind him, for this was his drying place for any wet clothes.

Now and then a pleasure boat was seen, and there were several canoes at some of the towns, but all of them flat-bottomed and open, and desperately unsafe—well named "péressoires." Some of these were made of metal, the use of which is a great mistake for any boat under ten tons, for in all such cases metal is much heavier than wood of the same strength, considering the strains which a boat must expect to undergo.

"La Ferté sous Jouarre" was the long of the next stopping place. There are several towns called by the name of La Ferté (La Fortifiée), which in some measure corresponds with the termination "caster" or "cester" of English names. Millstones are the great specialty of this La Ferté. A good millstone costs 50£, and there is a large exportation of them. The material has the very convenient property of not requiring to be chipped into holes, as these exist in this stone naturally. At La Ferté I put the boat into a hayloft; and at dinner with me there was an intelligent and hungry bourgeois from Paris, with his vulgar and hearty wife, and opposite to them the gossip of the town, who kept rattling on the stupid, endless fiddle-faddle of everybody's doings, sayings, failings, and earnings. Some amusement, however, resulted from the collision of two gossips at our table of four guests, for while the one always harped upon family tales of La Ferté, its local statistics, and the minute sayings of its people, the other kept struggling to turn our thoughts to shoes and slippers, for he was a commercial traveller with a cart full of boots. But after all, how much of our conversation in better life is only of the same kind, though upon larger, or at any rate other things; what would sound trifles to our British Cabinet might be the loftiest politics of Honolulu.

Starting early next day I felt an unaccountable languor; my arms were tired, and my energy seemed, for the first time, deficient. This was the result of a week's hard exercise, and of a sudden change of wind to the North. Give me our English climate for real hard work to prosper in. One generally associates the idea of north wind with cool and bracing air, and certainly in the Mediterranean it is the change of wind to the south, the hated *sirocco*, that enervates the traveller at once. But this north wind on the Marne came over a vast plain of arid land heated by two months of scorching sun, whereas the breezes of last week, though from the east, had been tempered in passing over the mountains of the Vosges. Forty-two miles lay before me to be accomplished before arriving tonight at my resting place for Sunday, and it was not a pleasant prospect to contemplate with stiff muscles in the shoulders. However, after twelve miles I found that some turnings of the river could be cut off by putting the boat on a cart, and thus a league of walking and 3*s*. 4*d*. of payment solved the difficulty. The old man with his cart was interesting to talk to, and we spoke about those deeper subjects which are of common interest to all.

At a turn in the road we came to a cart overturned and a little crowd round it, while the earth was covered with a pool of what seemed to be blood, but was only wine. The cart had struck a tree, and the wine cask on it had instantly burst, which so frightened the horse that he overset the cart. The Rob Roy was soon in the water again, and amid scenery much more enjoyable. I found an old soldier at a ferry who fetched me a bottle of wine, and then he and his wife sat in their leaky, flat, green-painted boat, and we all became very great friends. He had been at the taking of Constantine in Algeria, a place which really does look quite impossible to be taken by storm; but the appearance of a fortress is deceptive except to the learned in such matters. Who would think that the concealed fortress of Comorn, in Hungary, is stronger far than Constantine?

Meanwhile, a breeze has freshened up, and wafted me to Meaux, so that the day, begun with forebodings, ends as easy and as pleasant as the rest.

NOTES

1 In a little book lately published in France about the English Bar two facts are noted, that Barristers put the name of their "Inn" on their visiting cards, and that the Temple Volunteers are drilled admirably by a Serjeant-at-Law, who wields "an umbrella with a varnished cover, which glances in the sun like a sword!"

2 No permanent damage was done, and the Rob Roy afterwards went to Ireland, Scotland, and the North Cape in Norway. Now she rests in peace, "Emerita," the mother of at least 1000 boats built like her.

CHAPTER XV

Blacksmith—Holy Water—Quaint Questions—Unprotected Female—
Grave Gazers—Wrong Ways—The Boys, the Boys—Bends of the
Marne—Last Mooring—The Seine—Paris—Home.

Now rises the moon so clear, that we can't see a "man in the moon," but under the pale, quiet radiance there is a party of guests at a wedding dinner. The younger portion of the company adjourn to the garden and let off squibs and crackers, while some signal lights are shown from my window, and cheers resound as the Englishman illumines the neighbourhood! Next day the same people all assembled for the marriage breakfast, and Madeira and champagne flowed from the well-squeezed purse of the bride's happy father. The Germans had not come yet to Meaux.

One may notice that in a village the last sound to give way to the stillness of evening is that of the blacksmith's hammer, which is oftener heard abroad than at home. Perhaps this is because much of their execrable French ironwork is made separately in every town; whereas in England it is manufactured at special places by machinery. At any rate, after you have travelled on the continent long enough to become calm and observant, and to see, hear, and scent what is around, there is sure to be a picture in the memory full of blue dresses, white stones, jingling of bells, and the "cling, cling" of the never idle blacksmith.

This town of Meaux has a bridge with houses on it, and great millwheels filling up the arches as they did in old London Bridge. Pleasant gardens from the river, and the cafés glitter there at night. These are not luxuries but positive necessaries of life for the Frenchman, and it is the absence of these in new countries which is one chief cause why the Frenchman is so bad a colonist, for he has only the expression "with me" for "home," and no word for "wife" but "woman."

The cathedral of Meaux is grand and old, and see how they masquerade in the service in it! Look at the gaunt "Suisse," with his cocked hat kept on in church, and his sword and spear. The twenty priests and twelve red-surpliced boys intone to about as many hearers. A monk makes believe to sprinkle holy water on all sides from that dirty plasterer's brush, and then two boys carry on their shoulders a huge round loaf, the "pain benit," which, after fifty bowings, I blessed, and escorted back to be cut up, and is then given in morsels to the congregation. These endless ceremonies are the meshes of the net of Popery, and they are well woven to catch many French flies and other folks who must have action, show, the visible tangible outside, whatever may be meant by it.

Some form, of course, there must be in worship. One may suppose, indeed, that perfect spirit can adore God without attitude, or even any sequence or change. Yet in the Bible we hear of Seraphs veiling their bodies with their wings, and of Elders prostrate at certain times, and Saints that have a litany even in heaven. Mortals, too, must have some form of adoration, but there is the question, "How much?" and on this great point how many wise and foolish men have written books without end?

The riverside of the Marne was a good place for a quiet Sunday walk. Here a flock of 300 sheep had come to drink, and to nibble at the flowers hanging over the water, and the simple-hearted shepherd stood looking on while his dogs rushed backward and forward, evidently yearning for some sheep to do wrong, that their dog service might be required to prevent or to punish naughty conduct. This "Berger" inquires whether England is near Africa, and how large our legs of mutton are, and if we have sheepdogs, and are there any rivers in our island on the sea. Meanwhile at the hotel the marriage party kept on breakfasting, even until four o'clock, and non-melodious songs were sung. The French, as a people, do not excel in vocal music, either in tone or in harmony, but they are precise in time.

Afloat again next morning, and quite refreshed, we prepare for a long day's work. The stream was now clear, and the waving tresses of dark green weeds gracefully curved under water, while islands amid deep shady bays varied the landscape above. There are three hemispheres of scenery visible to the traveller who voyages thus in a boat on the river. First, the great arch of sky, and land, and trees, and flowers down to the water's brink; then the whole of this reflected beautifully in the surface of the river' and then again the wondrous depths in the water itself, with its animal life, its rocks and glades below, and its flowers and mosses underneath.

I saw a canal lock open, and paddled in merely for variety, passing soon into a tunnel, in the middle of which there was a huge boat fixed, and nobody with it. The boat exactly filled the tunnel, and the men had gone to their dinner, so I had first to drag their huge boat out, and then the canoe proudly glided into daylight, having a whole tunnel to itself. In the war this tunnel was blown up. At Lagny, where we meant to breakfast, I left the Rob Roy with a nice old gentleman, who was fishing in a nightcap and spectacles, and he assured me he would stop there two hours. But when I scrambled back to it through the mill (startling the miller's men among their wholesome dusty sacks), the disconsolate canoe was found all alone, the first time she had been left in a town an "unprotected female."

To escape a long serpent wind of the river, we entered another canal and found it about a foot deep, with clear water flowing pleasantly. This seemed to be very fortunate, and we enjoyed it most thoroughly, for a few miles, little knowing what was to come. But weeds began, then clumps of great rushes, then large bushes and trees, all growing with thick grass in the water, and at length this got so dense that the prospect before me was precisely like a very large hayfield, with grass four feet high, all ready to be mowed, but which had to be tediously rowed through. This on a hot day without wind, and in a long vista, unbroken by a man or a house, or anything lively, was rather daunting, but we had gone too far to recede with honour, and so by dint of pushing and working I actually got the boat through some miles of this novel obstruction (known only this dry summer), and brought her safe and sound again to the river.

At one place there was a bridge over this march, and two men happened to be going over it as the canoe came near. They soon called to some neighbours, and the row of spectators exhibited the faculty so notable in French people and so rarely found with us, that of being able to keep from laughing right out at a foreigner in an awkward case. The absurd sight of a man paddling a boat amid miles of thick rushes was indeed a severe test of courteous gravity. However, I must say that the labour required to penetrate this marsh was far less than one would suppose from the appearance of the place. The sharp point of the boat entered, and its smooth sides followed through hedges of aquatic plants, and, on the whole—after all was done—the trouble and muscular effort of this passage was better than the monotonous calm of sailing on a canal.[1]

Fairly in the broad river again, the *Rob Roy* came to Neuilly, and it was plain that my Sunday rest had enabled over thirty miles to be accomplished without any fatigue at the end. The canoe went to bed in a summer house, and her crew in a garret, where they could not stand upright—the only occasion where we were badly housed, misled by the sign of "The Jolly Rowers." Next day the river flowed fast again, and numerous islands made the channels very difficult to find. The worst of these troubles is that you cannot prepare for them. No map gives any just idea of your route, and the people on the river itself are profoundly ignorant of its navigation; for instance, in starting, my landlord told me that in two hours we should reach Paris; after ten miles an intelligent man said, "Distance from Paris? it is six hours from here;" while a third informed me a little further on, "It is just three leagues and a half from this spot."

The banks were now dotted with villas, and numerous pleasure boats were moored at neat little stairs. The vast number of these boats quite astonished me, yet very few of them were ever to be seen in actual use. The French are certainly ingenious in their boatmaking, but more of ingenuity than of practical exercise is seen on the water. On several rivers we remarked the "walking machine," in which a man can march on the water by fixing two small boats to his feet. A curious mode of rowing with your face to the bows has lately been invented by a Frenchman.[2]

We breakfasted at a new canal cutting, and as there were many *gamins* about, I fastened a stone to my painter, and so left the Rob Roy in the middle of the river, moored within sight of the arbour where I sat, and also within sight of the ardent-eyed boys who gazed for hours with wistful looks on the tiny craft. Their desire to handle as well as to see is only natural for these little fellows, and therefore, if the lads behave well, I always make a point of showing them the whole affair quite near, after they have had to abstain from it so long as a forbidden pleasure.

Strange that this quick curiosity of French boys does not ripen more of them into travellers, but it soon gets expended in trifling details of narrow circle, while the sober, sedate, nay, the *triste* Anglian is found scurrying over the world with a carpetbag, and pushing his way in foreign crowds without knowing one word of their language, and all the while as merry as lark. Among the odd modes of locomotion adopted by Englishmen, we have already mentioned that of the gentleman (now a member of the Canoe Club) who was travelling in Germany with a four-in-hand and two spare horses. We met another Briton who had made a tour in a road locomotive which he bought for 700*l.*, and sold again at the same price. One more John Bull, who regarded the canoe as a "queer conveyance," went himself abroad on a velocipede. None of these, however, could cross seas, lakes, and rivers like the canoe, wherever a man could walk or a plank could swim.

It seemed contrary to nature that, after thus nearing pretty Paris, one's back was now to be turned upon it for hours in order to have a wide, vague, purposeless voyage into country parts. But the river willed it so; for here a great curve began and led off to the left, while the traffic of the Marne went straight through a canal to the right—through a canal, and therefore the Rob Roy would not follow it there.

The river got less and less in volume; its water was used for the canal, and with its maimed strength it could scarcely trickle through a spacious sweep of country file; but now, since these lines were first written, the desperate sorties of Ducrot have flooded that channel with blood. In this long roundabout we were often grounded, or entangled in soft mossy weeds, or fastened in overhanging trees, and, in fact, suffered all the evils which the smallest brook could entail, though this was the bed of a mighty river. The bend of its course was more and more inexplicable as it turned more round and round, until my face was full in sunlight at noon, and I saw that the course was now due south. Rustics were there to look at me, and wondering herdsmen too, as if the boat was in mid Germany, instead of being close to Paris. Evidently boating men in that quarter never came here by the river, and the Rob Roy was a *rara avis* floating on a stream unused.

But the circle was rounded at last, as all circles are; and we got back to the common route, to civilization, fishing men and fishing women, and on open water in the broad Marne once more I stopped for a rest and a ponder.

And now we unmoor for the last time, and enter the Rob Roy for the last of more than a thousand miles we have paddled and sailed since our start. I will not disguise my feeling of sadness then, that the end had come so soon.

So when the murmuring stream glided into the Seine I found a cool bank to lie upon under the trees, with my boat gently rocking in the ripples below, and the near sound of a great city telling that Paris was at hand.

"Here," said I, "and now is my last hour of life savage and free. Sunny days, alone, but not solitary; worked, but not weary"—as in a dream the things, and places, and men I had seen for months of pleasant voyage now floated before my eyes half closed. The panorama was wide and fair to the inner sight; but it spoke forth a tale always the same as it rolled quickly past—that vacation was over, and work must begin.

Up, then, for this is not a life of mere enjoyment. Again into the harness of "polite society," the hat, the collar, the braces, the gloves, the waistcoat, the latchkey—perhaps, the razor—certainly the umbrella. How every joint and limb will rebel against these manacles, but they must be endured!

The gradual approach to Paris by gliding down the Seine was altogether a new sensation. By diligence, railway, or steamer, you have nothing like it—not certainly by walking into Paris along a dusty road. For now we are smoothly carried on a wide and winding river, with nothing to do but to look and to listen while the splendid panorama majestically unfolds. Villas thicken, gardens get smaller as houses are closer, trees get fewer as walls increase. Barges line the banks, commerce and its movement, luxury and its adornment, spires and cupolas grow out of the dim horizon, and then bridges seem to float towards me, and the hum of life gets deeper and busier, while the pretty little prattling of the river stream yields to the roar of traffic, and to that indescribable thrill which throbs the air around this the capital of the Continent, the centre of politics, the focus of pleasure, and splendour, and lies of the world.

The gradual approach to Paris by gliding down the Seine was altogether a new sensation. By diligence, railway, or steamer, you have nothing like it—not certainly by walking into Paris along a dusty road. For now we are smoothly carried on a wide and winding river, with nothing to do but to look and to listen while the splendid panorama majestically unfolds. Villas thicken, gardens get smaller as houses are closer, trees get fewer as walls increase. Barges line the banks, commerce and its movement, luxury and its adornment, spires and cupolas grow out of the dim horizon, and then bridges seem to float towards me, and the hum of life gets deeper and busier, while the pretty prattling of the river stream yields to the roar of the traffic, and to that indescribable thrill which throbs the air around this the capital of the Continent, the centre of politics, the focus of pleasure, and splendour, and lies of the world.

In passing the island at Notre Dame I fortunately took the proper side, but even then we found a very awkward rush of water under the bridges. This was caused by the extreme lowness of the river, which on this very day was three feet lower than in the memory of man. The fall over each barrier, though wide enough, was so shallow at the last bridge that the crowd above me evidently calculated upon my being upset; and they were nearly right too. The absence of other boats also showed that some great difficulty was at hand, but I remarked that by far the greater number of observers had collected over one particular arch, where at first there seemed to be the very worst chance for getting through.

By logical deduction I argued from this, "That arch must be the best after all, for they evidently expected me to try it," and, with a horrid presentiment that my first upset was to be at my last bridge, I boldly dashed forwards—whirl, whirl the waves, and grate—grate—my iron keel; but the Rob Roy rises to the occasion, and a rewarding Bravo! from the Frenchmen above is answered by a British "All right" from the Rob Roy below.

No town was so hard to find a place for the canoe in as this bright, gay Paris. We went to the floating baths; they would not have me. We paddled to the funny old ship; they shook their heads. We tried a coal wharf; but they were only civil there. Even the worthy washerwomen, my quondam friends, were altogether callous now about a harbour for the canoe. In desperation we paddled to a bath that was being repaired, but when my boat rounded the corner it was met by a volley of abuse from the proprietor for disturbing his fishing; he was in the act of closing in deadly struggle with a *goujon*.

Relenting at last as we told the Rob Roy's tale, he housed her there for the night; and I shouldered my luggage and walked to an hotel.

Here is Meurice's, with the homeward tide of Britons from every Alp and cave of Europe flowing through its salons. Here are the gay streets, too white to be looked at in the sun, and the *poupée* theatres under the trees, and the dandies so stiff in hired carriages, and the dapper little soldiers, and the tinkling horse bells, and the gilded cafés.

Yes, it is Paris—and more brilliant than ever!

I faintly tried to hope, but I could not believe that any person there had enjoyed his summer months with such delight as the captain, the purser, the ship's cook, and cabin boy of the Rob Roy canoe.

Eight francs take the boat by rail to Calais. Two shillings take her thence to Dover. The railway takes her free to Charing Cross, and there two porters put her in the Thames again.

A flowing tide, on a sunny evening, bears her fast and cheerily straight to Searle's, there to debark the Rob Roy's cargo safe and sound and thankful, and to plant once more upon the shore of Old England

> The flag that braved a thousand miles,
> The rapid and the snag.

NOTES

1 The remembrance of this afterwards enabled the Rob Roy to penetrate successfully the dense jungle of the vast marsh at the mouth of the Abana, east of Damascus.

2 Described in *The Voyage Alone in the Yawl Rob Roy* when our little three-ton yacht visited Paris for the Exhibition of 1867.

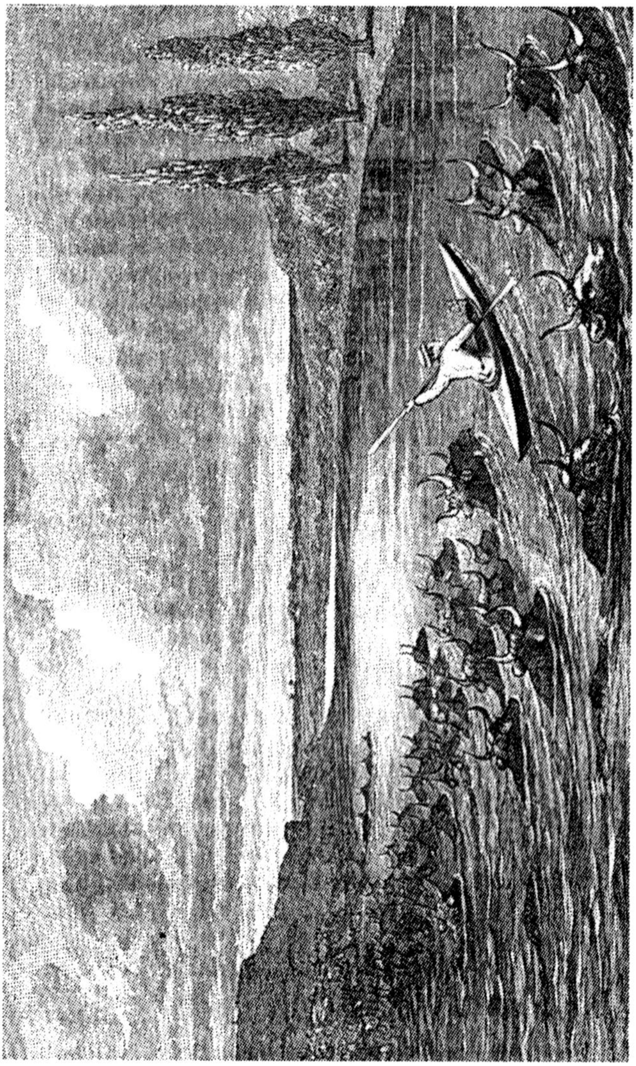